The Two Wars Of Red Black

Stuart L. Scott

Moscow, Idaho

The Two Wars of Red Black

Stuart L. Scott

Published by
Stuart L. Scott
112 S. Main St.
Moscow, Idaho

Copyright Stuart L. Scott, 2022

ISBN   Print 978-1-7375429-1-9
            e-Book 978-1-7375429-2-6

Printed by Ingram/Spark

All rights reserved, including the right to reproduce this book or any portion thereof in any form without the express written permission of the author.

Cover Design by: Tania Suarez Mendoza

This is a work of fiction. Many of the characters were inspired by historical research and the reminiscences of the main character, However, the events are fictionalized and do not represent actions attributable to any specific person living or dead.

Dedication:

And good night, Bill, Joyce and Clay, wherever you may be.

Contents

Introduction		vi
Prologue		1
1.	Stockton, California, 1933	3
2.	Stockton, California, 1942	5
3.	War Arrives for Red Black, 1941	7
4.	Kearns, Utah, June 1942	16
5.	Manhattan, Kansas, September 1942	19
6.	San Antonio Aviation Cadet Center, Texas, January 1943	25
7.	San Angelo, Texas, May 1943	26
8.	Casper, Wyoming, October 1943	29
9.	Topeka, Kansas and Across the Pond, January 1944	37
10.	AAC Hethel, England, February 1944	42
11.	Back in the Lion's Den, February 1944	54
12.	D-Day, June 6, 1944	59
13.	Catching Our Breath	69
14.	Vengeance Weapons, June 1944	71
15.	Somewhere in Denmark, August 1944	77
16.	Sweden, August 30 1944	92
17.	Between Two Wars, October 1945	100
18.	Change Is in the Wind, September 1947	106
19.	Orders for the Orient, April 1950	110
20.	December 1949	115
21.	Okinawa, May 1, 1950	125
22.	War, 1950	130
23.	We Shoot, August 1950 Above the Pusan Perimeter	132
24.	Pilot Down	135
25.	Late October 1950	141
26.	The Habu and the Mongoose	148
27.	November 1951	151
28.	Kojo, April 1952	155
29.	Florida, September 1952	165
30.	Moody AFB, Valdosta, GA	178
31.	Returning to Normal,1960	184
Epilogue		194
Afterword		195
Bibliography		198
About the Author		199
Also By This Author		200

Introduction

In 2017, a wildfire destroyed entire sections of Santa Rosa, California. When flames began lapping at the outside of my uncle's Assisted Living facility the residents were evacuated over grounds covered in fire-retardant. Family and friends all chipped in to provide housing, meals, transportation and necessary care for Uncle Bill.

At age 92, legally blind, diabetic and using a walker, he was unable to navigate airports and connecting flights on his own. His daughter put him on a flight to me. The fire retardant on his shoes shared constituents with improvised explosives, so the blind, hobbling veteran with vascular dementia was strip-searched for the good of us all. Thanks, TSA, for keeping us safe.

It was during Uncle Bill's three-week stay in my home when he finally started sharing details from his career that time and Alzheimer's had not stripped away. Every afternoon we shared a drink, his being dealcoholized wine, and mine a good red. I came prepared with a list of questions. Often my questions elicited answers that suggested other questions. Many times, my questions were answered by, "I can't remember."

I've used the information gained during those three weeks. I've researched my material to bring together the wheres, hows and whys. Why was he flying the two particular planes that featured prominently in his career? Why was he bombing Peenemünde, Germany?

I also had the benefit of reviewing a file containing all his orders received between 1949 and 1953, during the Korean War. I could place him at specific spots at specific times. This information I coordinated with what was happening in Korea, and how he may have been involved. So, my fiction has a basis in fact and in Red Black's presence. We are true as we can be to the actual events, based on available memory and records.

I've tried to paint a larger picture showing the 'whys' of American strategy that originated high above any flying officer. Please enjoy.

Prologue

In 1925, President Calvin Coolidge said, "The chief business of America is business." The Lend-Lease program began in the United States in January 1941. The aim of the program was to keep England afloat while simultaneously keeping America out of the war. But 'out of the war' was not synonymous with 'neutral.'

In exchange for 50 aging destroyers, America demanded leases for use of military bases, the plans for weapons under development and a license to produce the Rolls Royce Merlin airplane engine.

Our B-24 bomber was designed at the request of the Army Air Corps. The aircraft had a wing design that allowed both a heavy bomb load and larger fuel capacity. The Air Corps foresaw a war in the Pacific that would need a long-range bomber to deal with the greater flight distance in that theater of operations.

We were developing the P-51 Mustang as a long-range fighter escort for our bombers over Germany. For like reasons, the F-82 Twin Mustang had a flight range equal to our bombers pressing the war in the Pacific. Once again, the Army Air Corps foresaw a need and developed a plane to fill that need.

Hand in hand with the need for the B-24 was a need for trained crews to fly our planes. The wheels of bureaucracy began to turn, but too slowly for pilot and aircrew training facilities to be up and running by the time we were overtaken by the war. Private flying schools, public institutions and the military's own training facilities were linked to provide the multifaceted constellation of skills required to bring the Air Corps we'd need into action.

1. Stockton, California, 1933

It was going to be a hot August day in Stockton, my San Joaquin Valley town.

"Bill, if her father saw you doing that, he'd cut your dick off."

Bella Bacigalupo and I were so engrossed in playing doctor that my father's approach had escaped our notice. Dad's two hands clamped down on my shoulders, lifting me to standing. His grip pinioned my arms. As my feet cleared the ground, I desperately strained to pull up my underwear and jeans. The blame was going to be all mine.

"Bella, go home," Dad told my nine-year-old partner in crime. Her family's truck farm was across Cherokee Lane from Dad and Mom's chicken farm. His tone was commanding but kind. Bella and her twin sister Adelina were both 'fragile flowers in the hothouse of life,' in Dad's mind. The nine-year-old twins were 'early bloomers' or 'precocious,' as my mother described them.

My older sisters, Melba and Doris, had both left home for college or careers. Either I had been too young to care or they too modest for me to ever gain any first-hand observation of the full female anatomy.

"Everyone has been looking for you two. We were about to drag the canal." Finally, the vise grip on my shoulders released, and we walked side by side up the gravel shoulder that skirted Cherokee Lane. The first heat waves of the day shimmered just above the strip of asphalt. We walked in silence except for the occasional passing car and the rhythmic crunch of gravel under his boots and my Chuck Taylor high-top canvas shoes.

As I walked in silence, the first whiffs of tar rising from the warming asphalt mingled with the ever-present odor of chicken manure. The aroma always seemed to circle my father like his own personal cloud. I heard in my mind Dad's often repeated mantra, "You can't make chicken salad out of chicken shit," followed by Mom's predictable response: "Verrall, couldn't you please just say manure?"

"Son, do you know what Bacigalupo means?"

Should I repeat what Bella told me as part of our private show and tell? It means a tasty mouthful. But I didn't give voice to her words as Dad continued.

"It's two words: 'baci,' that's kiss, and 'lupo,' the wolf. Now how do you suppose a wolf kisses? With a gentle lick? Or," he paused, heightening the drama, "with its teeth?"

Glancing over, he smiled broadly, showing his own teeth. With a quick flash of his eyes and a feigned head move in my direction, he snapped his jaws in an audible bite.

I winced. His message had been received.

2. Stockton, California, 1942

My Father's Scotch-Irish forebearers were mercenaries for Oliver Cromwell. It was steadier work than blackmailing and cattle thieving in the Scottish midlands. Our family came to the new world: Ireland to Canada and down into the United States; New York to Iowa, then Nevada. After a 1920 fire burned our entire Nevada town, Stockton, California became our home.

According to my father, taxes were the Devil's work and Franklin Roosevelt was the Devil. The Scots and the Irish are quick to remember how they suffered at English hands.

While not an admirer of Adolph Hitler, Dad admired the Germans for their work ethic. He hoped our national hero, Charles Lindbergh, would oppose Roosevelt in the next presidential election. Since the December 7th attack on Pearl Harbor, I hoped for a change in his attitude. But it hadn't happened yet.

"All Orientals are sneaky bastards, except maybe the Chinks like old man Wong who had the laundry back in Deeth," he would say, and spit tobacco juice. But war in Europe was another thing. "Now the Germans are just getting back what the Limeys and the Frogs grabbed after the last war."

My Mom kept quiet, and I did too, right until the moment that I told the old man I'd decided to enlist in Army Air Corps.

Edward Verrall Black, Sarah Belknap Black, Doris Black, William Black

Since my junior year at Stockton High, I worked after school at Johnny Crosetti's drug store. After graduation, he promoted me to chief soda jerk and part-time delivery boy. Mr. Crosetti hung the nickname "Red" on me because of my red hair. I liked the nickname better than being called "Jug-head" by the other guys on the school baseball team.

The Crosetti family had moved from San Francisco to Stockton. Their son, Frankie Crosetti, was the 'honest-to-gosh' shortstop for the New York Yankees. In the off season, he'd hang out at the drugstore soda fountain when he came to visit his folks. Last year, he brought along three friends from the old neighborhood in San Francisco. Vince, Joe and Dom DiMaggio were all playing in the outfield for the San Francisco Seals and hoping to join Frankie in 'the bigs.' The biggest thrill I'd ever had, at least with my clothes on, was Frankie showing me the secrets of his position and batting balls to me at Memorial Field.

"Listen Red, you've got talent. Work on those positioning tricks and ways of reading the batters until next time I'm back in Stockton. I'll see where you are then and see about getting a Yankee's scout to look you over. Stay in touch. Fair enough?"

"Wow, that would be great, Mr. Crosetti," I answered as we loaded balls, bat and gloves into my gear bag.

"It's Frankie to you, kid. Mr. Crosetti is my old man."

3. War Arrives for Red Black, 1941

San Francisco Chronicle, December 9, two days after Pearl Harbor.

"Rumors of enemy carriers off the California coast and unidentified aircraft over the Bay Area led to the closing of schools in San Francisco and Oakland. Civil defense wardens enforced a blackout. Local radio stations maintained radio silence from 10 a.m. until 9 p.m. Monday night. Federal authorities deemed the reports of an impending attack credible. From his headquarters at the Presidio, Lt. General John L. DeWitt, head of our Coast Defense District, discounted the claims by critics of a reaction based on war nerves.

"Last night there were planes over this community. Enemy planes! Japanese planes! And we tracked them out to sea," General DeWitt told the public ominously. "I am confident the Army can stop any Japanese landing on the west coast, either at the Sierra Nevada Mountains or the Grand Canyon."

February of 1942 was a pivotal month; the West Coast came under attack. Attu in the Aleutian Islands was occupied. Firebombs landed in Oregon forests. Victoria Harbor in Canada and Fort Stevens, at the mouth of the Columbia River, were shelled. Almost daily, the drumbeat of war grew louder in our ears.

One day, an oil tanker was torpedoed inside Monterey Bay, only 150 miles from Stockton. Would they sail up the 600-foot-wide Stockton Shipping canal from Suisun Bay and shell us next? If cargo ships could make the journey, so could troop ships. As our physical separation from the war decreased, our ability to keep it at arm's length vanished.

On February 23rd, my sister Doris was working at the Tidewater Oil Company's Ellwood facility. A Japanese submarine trying to shell fuel storage tanks destroyed a derrick and pumphouse at the facility. The following night, she sat in the dark listening to anti-aircraft guns firing up into an empty sky and the shrapnel landing on civilian homes.

"The Battle of Los Angeles" was how Hearst and Pulitzer newspapers described the 'war nerves' panic that cost six civilian lives.

My folks and I listened to the big Emerson console radio in our front room. As we listened to the litany of bad news, I realized how the distant wars had come home to them, even in Stockton. Mom always sat close to Dad. His hearing was lousy, so he always talked too loudly, unaware of his own volume. Hearing their conversation didn't require eavesdropping. I listened.

"If they land on the coast, load what you can in the truck and head for Elko. We ought to be safe in Nevada, but we can't stay here."

That was the moment that I decided it was time to enlist.

Doris Black, William Black, Melba Black

I needed to find someone who could give me advice on how to wind up in the Army Air Corps instead of being drafted into the infantry. And I knew where to go. Stockton Field was home to the West Coast Army Air Corps Training Center.

I took a city bus across town to the airfield gate, now festooned with sandbagged machine gun positions and patrolled by armed guards. I told a gate guard I wanted to enlist. "Who can I talk to?"

He didn't know. "Wait here and I'll call base operation. They'll know who you should see," instructed the sentry. He pointed me to a place to wait, under an open bus shelter out of the sun. The familiar sounds of passing traffic began to blend with the drone of the base. I kept my eyes on him and watched him place the call. Hanging up the phone, he gestured me back to the guard shack. "Major Moen will come out and get you. He'll tell you what you need. Good luck, kid."

I replied my thanks.

I was watching for either an olive-drab jeep or maybe a black staff car. What I got instead was a solitary figure dressed in plain khaki, wearing a garrison cap adorned with a gold oak leaf. The guard saluted the man, pointed to me and after a nod from the Major, motioned me over.

As we walked deeper into the interior of Stockton field, I could distinguish the rhythmic drumming of feet marching in unison. Off to my right, I glimpsed a runway. The roars of airplane engines added to the symphony of sounds.

Major Moen confirmed why I was there. He listened to my request for information as we walked back to his office inside a two-story wood frame building. Once behind his desk, he removed his cap and placed it in a desk drawer. "Sit down," he said and indicated either of the two wooden chairs across the desk.

He laid out the steps involved and arranged a date for me to take the Army General Classification Test (AGCT) entrance exam to determine my career choices. I'd take the test in three days, there at Stockton field. Major Moen said he'd review my options after I had my test scores. Then he stood up, signaling that our meeting was over, and said he'd walk me back to the main gate.

I thanked him and followed him outside. As we walked, I asked him a question. "Sir, are you any relation to the Moen plumbing supply company?"

"Yes, that is my family's business. My dad started out as a humble plumber and then got into plumbing supplies," he smiled, and I nodded. At the gate, he offered his hand for a shake.

"Sir, can I ask why you didn't stay in the family plumbing supply business?"

"Bill, the first thing my father told me about the plumbing business was," and he paused, smiling. "Never chew your nails."

* * * *

I met again with Major Moen several days later. "Bill, you did well on the test. I'm impressed." He reached across the desk offering me a congratulatory handshake. I'm sure relief showed on my face.

"You are eligible for all the flight crew training programs. I haven't always been behind a desk. I was a fighter pilot during the last war." I leaned forward as the solemnity amped up. "Listening to you, I get the impression you are a serious young man. We need good people, serious people, who are willing to put themselves on the line for the good of our country." His gaze dropped to the desktop for a moment. Then he looked straight back at me. "And for the good of the world. If you are the man I think you are, I'll enlist you here and now." And he paused again.

"Or, if you want your folks here to see you sworn in, we'll do that tomorrow. Your call."

The decision was mine to make. I had no mental reservation and answered straight away. "Sir, my folks are starting to see how we are in danger right now. My sister Doris works at the facility in Santa Barbara that the Japs just shelled. I don't want to see any of our enemies coming up the ship canal. I'm sure as hell not giving up our west coast to anyone.

"Enlist me now, please."

He made no audible response to my decision but pressed an intercom button on his desktop. "Sergeant Brooks."

"Yes sir," responded the voice.

"I need an enlistment form package and for you to witness my administering the Oath of Enlistment to Bill Black."

Adrenaline filled my veins at the sea change my life was about to take. I sat erect and my mouth felt dry. The sounds from beyond the window no longer registered with me.

The sergeant knocked before entering. He placed forms before me on the Major's desk. "Bill, read the top page before you sign," and he pushed a desk set pen around to face me.

No one spoke as I leaned forward, scrutinizing the document.

When I finally signed my name, Major Moen stood up and came around the desk. I rose from my seat and Sergeant Brooks snapped to attention.

The Major instructed me, "Raise your right hand and repeat after me. 'I, William James Black, do solemnly swear that I will support and defend the United States against all enemies, foreign and domestic; that I will bear true faith and allegiance to the same; and that I will obey the orders of the President of the United States and orders of officers appointed over me, according to regulations and the Uniform Code of Military Justice.'"

* * * *

My hand had gone up. I'd sworn the enlistment oath. I was in the army. What now?

"Private Black, congratulations."

"Thank you," I replied.

"Now, go home."

What the hell? I lowered my arm to my side. My excitement and my understanding of what was happening both plummeted. Finally, I spoke. "Sir?"

Major Moen went back to his seat and Sergeant Brooks returned to his work. I stood, waiting and trying to understand what I was supposed to do next. Finally, the Major motioned for me to sit.

"Private, we are less than three months into a war. Frankly, we are hugely unprepared. We need good men like you. But we also need to prepare our system for the influx that will be coming." Silent for a few moments, he drummed his fingertips on the desktop before continuing.

He wasn't smiling now, his expression somewhere between neutral and grim. "I've got nothing for you here. No bed, no uniform and no training. Those essential elements of turning civilians into airmen are all being developed as I speak. Go home, son. Tell your folks that you are awaiting orders and the start of the next training cycle."

"Yes sir."

"Ok, now go home. Sergeant Brooks will contact you when we are ready."

* * * *

I did as I was told and waited at home. I asked my folks to avoid the topic as best they could. I brought sisters Melba and Doris into the information loop. We'd only say that I'd enlisted and was waiting to ship out.

Three months after I put up my hand and swore the oath, a letter from Sergeant Brooks arrived. I was to show up at the Western Pacific depot in 5 days' time.

"You may bring one bag with a change of underwear, razor, tooth-brush, comb, prescription medications, and up to $5 cash." Also included was a longer list of what was not allowed: "illegal drugs, weapons, pornography, gambling devices such as dice, pictures larger than wallet size, books or toys."

Really, no toys? The letter did not say where I was going or when I would get there.

I kissed Mom goodbye at the house. Melba skipped her job in the county public health lab to say her good-byes. Dad drove me to the train station. Sitting across from him in the cab of his truck, I shook his hand and got out. I joined the group of men, each with his bag, waiting by the empty tracks. Fellas my age mixed with men years older. White and brown faces were forming into small islands of color under the noon-day sun.

I search the growing crowd for familiar faces and found several. There was Eddie Arroyo, my teammate on the Stockton High varsity baseball team. 'Fast Eddie' as we called him, was our fleet-footed center fielder. Eddie was already talking with Chris and Craig, two other guys from school. I joined their group, happy to have some friends to help me face whatever unknowns were ahead.

Two shrill blasts from an approaching locomotive interrupted our conversation. The hiss of steam and squeal of brakes brought everything to a halt. A conductor appeared, clad in the familiar blue serge uniform with a flat-topped, black-brimmed cap. He came down the three steps from a passenger car entrance, a small metal step stool in one hand, and jumped down to the asphalt already baking in the June sun.

Setting the stool down, he nudged it with his polished black shoe to a spot aligned with the passenger car steps. He clasped a loop of chain hanging from a vest pocket and withdrew a bright brass whistle. His loud, long whistle blast ended. "Board!"

And we did.

Our groups formed into lines as each man mounted the four steps to an unknown future. A second conductor at the top of the stairs gave directions. "Go all the way through the vacant cars. Fill every seat from the back; no spaces."

I passed through three empty passenger cars. Inside the fourth car, the back half was already full of other men also bound for basic training. No conductor here; instead, a uniformed sergeant stood with his back to the entrance aisle.

"Take the first available seat. Be quiet and put bags under your seat or in the rack above. Keep moving." His tone was neither friendly nor threatening. It was just business.

4. Kearns, Utah, June 1942

Thirty-six hours later, our train arrived at our destination. Where, we didn't know. The overhead lights flared to bright as we rolled to a stop. It was late in the evening and as the engine noises quieted, I heard crickets chirping somewhere off in the dark.

We'd finished the journey's fourth box-lunch meal three hours before. These gourmet delights were unvarying, regardless of the meal. One slice of American cheese sandwiched between buttered white bread slices. A baseball-size red apple and two cookies for desert completed each meal. The sandwiches and cookies had probably started out fresh, I hoped. At least the offered carton of white milk was cold and the coffee hot: mostly.

I nudged Fast Eddie awake and we both stared out the window. I hoped it didn't show, but inside I was scared. This was my first time out of Stockton. I was glad to have a friend at my side. Bright flood lights shone down onto a row of gray buses parked nose to tail beside the train. Each bus had "Kearns Army Air Corps Base" neatly painted on its side.

"Everybody up, grab your shit and get off," shouted our uniformed escort. Compliant as lambs to the slaughter, we grabbed our stuff and filed off the train. Waiting outside each train car was another sergeant, his khaki uniform crisply ironed. A flat-brimmed Stetson Standard campaign hat crowned his head.

"Get on the bus, all the way to the back," was his mantra. And we did. No overhead racks here, so any bags or suitcases not crammed under seats rode on our laps. As quickly as the buses filled, they were off into the dark. The sergeant boarded last and stood behind the driver as we moved.

No town here, just headlights slicing the night. Finally, a glow appeared in the distance. It sharpened into focus, revealing a perimeter fence lit by downward-facing flood lights, each engulfed in a cloud of swarming insects. A guarded, gated portal marked the end of the road. The sign above the gate: Kearns Army Air Corps Base. And in we went, beautiful dreamers all. The bus rolled to a stop on a large, paved pad, and the Sergeant was first off.

"Get off my bus," he screamed, over and over until the last man was off. Our eyes were wide, and I wondered what I had done.

"Fall in. Form up opposite me, arms-length from the man on your right and the man in front," he commanded loudly but no longer screaming. Holding one arm out in front and his other arm out to the right, he showed what was expected of us. And we did. Sergeants from each bus strode back and forth in front of their assigned flocks.

"Close ranks." No instruction now, and with only an instant of hesitation, we closed. "My name is Sergeant Bradford. I am your Drill Sergeant. The first word out of your mouth will be, 'Sir.'" Screaming again, "Do you understand?"

And a ragged chorus of "Sir, yes, sir!" or a nonsensical "Sir, yes," followed. Bradford prowled the thirty-man formation, firmly moving men up or over, until our order suited his expectation of acceptable Army form. And off we marched toward the black shapes of buildings across the paved parade ground.

Outside a tarpaper-covered two-story building in a sandy courtyard, Bradford's shout stopped us. "Company halt. Right face." We were looking at the doors in the center of a barracks, where another Sergeant stood.

"Listen up," Bradford said. "You will now be assigned bunks. As I call your name, head into the barracks. Sgt. Coats will give you your room and bunk assignment."

He paused and shifted gears. "If you hear, 'FIRE-FIRE-FIRE,' you will exit immediately. Is that clear?"

"Sir, yes, sir!" repeated from 30 voices. At the sound of our names, we entered. Sgt. Coats gave each man a room and bed number.

"Lights out in five minutes," and true to the announcement, in five minutes, the lights extinguished.

Two hours later, they sprung the first surprise. "FIRE-FIRE-FIRE," and the building emptied.

Barefoot, in our underwear, we stood in formation and waited for Bradford and Coats to appear. Somewhere behind me came the unmistakable sound of a healthy urine stream hitting the ground. I bit my lip to suppress a laugh. So began my first shitty day at Camp Kearns, Utah.

* * * *

Three months of Basic Training followed. Days one and two were filled with initiation procedures: clothing issue, haircuts, medical and dental inspections and the like. We were herded into an auditorium and received our "Dear Mom" cards.

Its brief message began, "Dear…" and we filled in the "I have arrived safely at Camp Kearns, Utah. I am fine and being well treated. I will write when I can. In the meantime, I can receive mail with my name and training unit number…" and the card had a space for our training company number. The card concluded with the general mailing address for Kearns.

Our routine: shit-shower-and-shave, clean the barracks and calisthenics, all before breakfast. Then marching, more calisthenics, running, classes and shots. We saw the camp being built out around us to its ultimate capacity of several thousand men. Marching to the sergeant's called cadence joined the ever-present background sounds of hammers and saws. The tarpaper buildings multiplied and filled with more recruits during my three months.

For some, learning to get along with people of different backgrounds and how to follow directions may have been new. Not so to me. I already knew how to make my bed, sew and shine shoes, but I did gain practice at standing in lines. I was no longer a civilian. After sewing on my first set of stripes, marking me as a Private Second Class, I was put on a bus for my next stop.

5. Manhattan, Kansas, September 1942

Manhattan, Kansas, I summed up for my dad in a single word: "flat." If the earth was ever going to get an enema, I now knew where the tube would be inserted.

We were now students on a college campus. Educational institutions had been brought into the business of training our fighting forces. Fast Eddie Arroyo, Chris and Craig were my classmates. Here I would spend the next eleven weeks learning a variety of skills and trying to become a navigator.

The first morning found us seated in a campus auditorium. At center stage, an Army officer introduced himself as Major Hansen, commander of the campus Reserve Officer Training Corps staff. He and his cadre were also in change of the Army Air Corps students. He announced that AAC cadets had a daily formation with the ROTC. Uniform inspections, group calisthenics and runs kept us in a military mindset.

What were we doing here? It was a little bit of training in the multiple disciplines which might be needed after classification. We got our first exposures to meteorology, celestial navigation, radio navigation, map reading and flying. Flight Officer Classification would come later, at San Antonio, Texas.

"Now, sit back and watch the following training film. After the film you are dismissed," directed Major Hansen. A theater screen lowered from the ceiling. His podium disappeared as the auditorium lights went out.

* * * *

"Donut Dolly or Lounge Lizard," the title filled the screen. A deep voice announced, "Just like overseas, enemy identification is key to your survival. Learn to recognize your enemy," and the film opened into a Hollywood-produced dramatization.

The scene begins with two cadets, off post for the first time, in the downtown of Anywhere USA. Up ahead, two large signs come into view. "USO," reads one large red on white sign. Two doors down the street, a neon cocktail glass glows under the name, "The Green Lantern."

Our two Cadets predictably make different choices and agree to meet back on post that night. Inside the USO we watch our hero, "Cadet Smart," having a coffee and a donut with a fresh-faced girl who sips a coke. Her blonde hair rings a well-scrubbed face. Her dress looks just like his kid sister's Sunday go-to-church frock. They laugh and share a dance, then another. She listens as he describes his Nebraska home, his folks and his beloved old dog Shep.

In the background, a clock hand winds away three pleasant hours. The young innocents part at the door as they share a hug. Their dialogue concludes with, "You come back any time, soldier. I'll be saving you a dance. Stay safe now," and our scene fades to black.

Down the block, "Cadet Stupid" is met inside the dimly lit interior by a red-lipped brunette wearing an oriental silk dress. One thigh is visible through a revealing slit. "Enemy identification — friend or foe — watch and see," says the announcer.

Removing a cigarette from her mouth, she smiles at our cadet, and her siren song begins. As she leads him to a table, the clock above registers the time. She smiles and asks, "Want to buy me a drink, soldier?"

He loosens his tie, and we watch his predictable descent into degradation. Drink follows drink as the clock's hour hand trails behind the steadily revolving minute hand. There are titters and catcalls from the audience as Cadet Stupid follows the 'princess of darkness' upstairs into her web of depravity. OH NO! And the scene fades to black.

We open next on our two intrepid cadets standing with their backs to us at adjoining urinals. Cadet Stupid audibly winces as he experiences the first tinge of pain. Our hero, ever concerned, innocently asks, "What wrong?"

"I don't know, Jimmy, but I feel like I'm pissing fire," and Stupid clutches the piping as his pain increase.

"You better go on sick call, Sam, and get yourself looked at. You can't be up in our plane with that pain."

The scene fades to black, reopening as Stupid Sam sits shamefaced across from an Army doctor who's giving him the bad news.

"I'm afraid that you have a venereal disease and will be out of action for some time. Hopefully, we've caught it early enough, so there will be no permanent damage." As the doctor lectures Sam, he busies himself filling a large syringe. Perhaps the needle only looks six inches long.

"Permanent damage?" asks Sam, his voice quivering.

"Yes, I'm afraid so. Permanent sterility, blindness, even insanity if it's left untreated."

Sam winces at the totally unforeseen bad news. OH NO!

"But don't worry, this shot should do the trick," and the smiling Doc approaches Sam, veterinary-size syringe in hand. We fade to black.

Our movie ends as our narrator describes the preventative or prophylactic uses of a Pro-Station.

A poster showed a cartooned soldier wearing a pointed dunce cap writing on a blackboard, "I should have gone to the Pro-Station, over and over. Under it was a small table with an open wood box filled with condoms and brown paper packets. "E. P. T. — PRO-KIT, Individual Chemical Prophylactic (For Protection from Venereal Disease)."

Holding up the packet, an unseen person reads the contents: "1) Tube containing 5 grams of ointment; 2) Instruction sheet; 3) Soap-impregnated cloth; 4) Cleansing tissue."

"The Army loses about 600 soldiers per day to the clap. These are free condoms that the guys can take before going off post. The E.P.T. packets are here just in case you forgot to wrap your rascal. If you think you may have dipped your pen in the wrong ink, use one of these. Squeeze the ointment into your penis, massage it up inside and hope that it beat the bugs."

* * * *

On our first free weekend, Eddie and I went into the nearby town of Manhattan and found a sporting goods store. Cadets were required to stay in uniform when off the campus, so we were easy to spot. October in Kansas was almost as hot as Stockton, so we finished our cokes outside and set the bottles down before entering.

"Hello, fellas. What can I do for you today?" the middle-aged store clerk asked, seeing our eyes searching the store.

"Baseball gloves and a couple of balls," Fast Eddie said.

The clerk motioned for us to follow and led us to the correct display.

"Right- or left-handed?"

"Right," we both replied.

"You're in luck. I've got all these styles for you. Any particular positions? Catcher's mitt, first baseman or general fielder's gloves?"

"Fielder's gloves," I said, and Eddie nodded in agreement.

In response, the clerk gestured to the bottom row of eight gloves. Wilson or Rawlings brands were ours for the choosing.

"Go ahead and try them on; check the feel and see if you like the style of webbing."

I immediately went to a three-finger Rawlings. Turning my back to the clerk and Fast Eddie, I held the glove to my face and inhaled the smell of new leather. It was a small moment that took me back to Stockton and safer times, if for just an instant.

Fast Eddie grabbed a four-fingered Wilson, his preferred style for playing the outfield. He pounded the pocket with his fist, testing the leather. We both checked the prices and exchanged glances, shocked to see bigger numbers than we expected. The clerk caught our looks and guessed what we were thinking.

"More than you thought? Leather is expensive because the government is buying it all." We confirmed his suspicions with nods and shrugs and put the gloves back on the display. I was about to ask if there was a second-hand store in town where a bargain might be found, when he spoke up.

"I can tell you're both aviation cadets getting trained over at the college." He was smiling at us now in what seemed a sad way. What his smile could not convey, his eyes seemed to reveal.

"How much have you got between you?" And we checked our thin wallets and gave the number: about 60 percent of the ticketed prices.

"Close enough," he said and handed each of us his chosen glove. Then he took what money we had to spend. His face grew tighter as his smile broke into a sigh. The backstory behind his smile remained untold. Our own smiles and handshakes offered in return were small payment for his kindness.

He stepped away briefly, his back turned. I saw one hand briefly rise to his face and wipe his eyes. Turning back towards us, he held out two baseballs and a small tin of glove oil.

"You'll need these to get the pockets shaped," was all he said, the same sad smile on his face. My throat tightened. Unable to speak a proper good-bye, we returned his smile with our own simple "Thanks," and walked out into the bright Kansas sun.

I glanced back at one of his front windows. There on display, a small satin pennant, suspended from a gold wooden rod, hung on a braided gold cord. One gold star and one blue star. Beneath the hanging pennant, sitting on the display window floor, was a silver trophy next to a framed picture of a boy in a baseball uniform, holding a bat.

"Eddie, come look at this." We both stood transfixed by what we saw. It explained so much. "Red, come on, we know what we have to do." I understood and followed my friend back into the store. Our recent benefactor turned toward us when he heard the door close. We exchanged no words when we snapped to attention and saluted the father who'd already contributed one son to the war effort and still risked another.

* * * *

Back on campus later that afternoon, I began rubbing oil into the glove leather. Then, placing my new ball inside, I tied the glove shut with some scavenged string to shape the pocket. I imagined that Fast Eddie was doing the same with his beautiful new Wilson. I wrote my folks, "Please ask Johnny Crosetti to tell Frankie that I have a glove and am practicing my skills."

At morning chow, I caught up with Fast Eddie. "What's on our dance card today?"

"Ah. Today my friend, we make our first venture into the sky, like the flyers we signed up to be. We start as 'ride-alongs'." Fast Eddie dreamed of becoming a pilot and had been waiting for his first time aloft. He seemed to vibrate with excitement.

One of the gray buses awaited us at the edge of the campus commons. A ten-minute ride later, 30 cadets piled off the bus and waited in formation for instructions.

Parked along the runway were six, two-seater training planes. Second Lieutenant Billie Ellis, clipboard in hand, approached and announced the training schedule. So began 60 hours of ride-along flights in the front seat of a Porterfield 65 trainer.

The thirty-minute flights started straight and level but gradually changed. More turns, ups and downs provided our first-hand experience to see if we were prone to air sickness. "Don't puke in my plane," was a common order from our smiling trainers, some of whom seemed intent on creating a violation of their own rule. My only involuntary emptying came after an emergency landing in a corn field. Not bad for a farm kid who'd never been higher than a county fair Ferris wheel.

After our four months in Manhattan, most of us moved on. Our next train ride brought us to San Antonio, Texas, for AAC Classification.

6. San Antonio Aviation Cadet Center, Texas, January 1943

San Antonio was an active duty AAC base. Lots of saluting, traffic and khaki. We began our first full day as always, watching the "Donut Dolly" cautionary film again.

Upon arrival, we were all slated for pilot training. Only after washing out as pilots did these guys even consider being navigators or bombardiers.

Unlike most of the cadets, I applied to be a navigator. Less chance of starting my military career with a failure.

And our testing began.

There were visual acuity tests, psychomotor tests to measure coordination, and advanced testing on lessons from Manhattan, like map reading, celestial navigation and meteorology.

Playing catch with Fast Eddie was a tremendous respite for my spirit at the end of each training day. We both thought our time was better spent with baseball than booze and bullshit.

At the end of these three months our promotions to Private First Class came through. I had qualified for pilot, bombardier or navigator, and at my request, they selected me for navigators' school. Chris and Craig went across town for pilot training at Randolph Field.

A hot and dusty five-hour bus ride followed as my tour of Texas continued.

7. San Angelo, Texas, May 1943

The San Angelo Army Airfield would be my duty station for the next six months. Fast Eddie was on the same bus with me but headed for bombardier training. Upon arrival, we began the next full day and watched "Donut Dolly" again.

We had liberty after each day of training ended. On Monday, Navigator Class # 44-4 with the 34th Flight Training Wing began. The principal activity at San Angelo was bombardier training. Nearby wide-open spaces allowed cordoned–off bomb ranges. The entire base was constantly under its own background din of revving engines and squealing tires. The faint aroma of aviation fuel was our constant companion.

Multiple B-25 Mitchells, B-17 Flying Fortresses and B-24 Liberators were present. These planes were to be our in-flight classrooms.

Fast Eddie and I continued to meet after our training day to play catch and share our latest training or news from home. We met by a pop machine outside the base PX. He had received news clippings from home about Bob Hope doing a USO show at Stockton Field.

Eddie told me the inside story about our prize weapon, the Norden bombsight. "Episode One of the 'Great Norden Saga.' They say it can drop a bomb into a pickle barrel from 30,000 feet," he announced with great solemnity as befitted such an invention. "It is undoubtedly one of man's greatest inventions next to canned beer and condoms.

"Now, in Episode Two, we get the 'buts'."

"Like what?" I inquired.

Straight-faced as always, Fast Eddie continued. "Little things can cause our secret weapon to not hit shit: clouds, extreme cold, darkness or high winds. Shall I go on?"

And I replied, "Why not?"

"Extreme turbulence, evasive maneuvers to avoid or fighters," and he stopped, still smiling. "Little things, but other than that, the Norden is great!"

We sat in silence for a while, sipping our sodas. "Now, lest you feel that our government wasted a shit-load of money, here is some good news," and he smiled, "at least for me personally. See, in daylight raids like we are doing, we fly in a tight formation. Mutual protection. The bombardier in the lead plane, theoretically the best bombardier in the whole damn outfit, aims and drops his bombs and we all do the same, on his signal."

Now it was my turn. "Okay, here's the scoop on navigating one of these big silver bastards."

"Lay it on me, Mr. Bones."

While it was hard to beat the Norden story, I could at least try. "We fly by following a radio beam sent from England that points us to our target. The beam sends a tone to the pilots and the navigator. If the pilot veers off the beam to the left, he gets a Morse code 'N' signal, 'dah-dit.' Off to the right, he hears an 'A' signal, 'dit-dah'."

Fast Eddie considered my revelation before speaking. "If you're not feeding the pilot navigation instructions, then what are you doing all this time?"

"Mostly I handle the 'thumb-in-the-ass' department."

"No seriously, why do we even have an on-board navigator if you are as useless as tits on a boar hog?"

I raised my hand, index finger pointed to the sky. "I am there in case our radio gets shot out or fails. Or if we have to divert to make an escape. Anything unforeseen. I am the manual back-up when the technology or our plan goes to shit."

"And if that doesn't happen?"

"Well then, I have a delightful view looking at my chart table or up at the Co-pilots back. If I'm not serving coffee and donuts to crew."

Fast Eddie leaned over and shook my one free hand. "But hey, unless you're in the lead plane, your very own bombardier can help you with the drink service!"

I smiled back, and we clicked soda bottles about the secrets we could tell but wouldn't.

Fast Eddie and I graduated together. We were commissioned as Second Lieutenants and pinned on the single gold bars of our grade.

8. Casper, Wyoming, October 1943

Casper Army Airfield was an Army training command base. I would spend the next three months there. Here newly trained pilots, navigators, bombardiers, flight engineers and gunners were formed into flight crews. I was about to meet those guys who would become nine of my closest friends. We would live together, fight together, and possibly die together. Predictably, we again watched Cadet Stupid learn about Enemy Identification, the clap and Pro-Stations.

The loudspeaker blared, "All arriving officers will report to the post theater at 0800 tomorrow for assignment."

We filled the seats and waited. The buzz of conversation overshadowing the auditorium halted when a single speaker took his place behind the lectern at center stage. He touched the big silver microphone, an audible "tap-tap-tap" that silenced the room.

"Good morning." The officer wore the Silver Oak Leaves of a Lieutenant-Colonel. "When you hear your name and the last four digits of your service number, join your assigned group at the back of the auditorium." Without further explanation, our sorting into crews began.

"I'll catch up with you tonight at our quarters, after we're all sorted into crews," said Fast Eddie.

"Yeah" was all I had time to say before 'Arroyo-1634' was called.

Soon my name was called. I was assigned to Group Six, already forming in the back of the auditorium. While names were being called and men moving, I introduced myself to the other four men already together. Frank McGuffey, Horace Hawkins, Bill Frisbee and Jim Rhodes. Frank, with the silver bar of a first lieutenant on his collar, was our senior officer and lead pilot, Horace was his co-pilot. Jim Rhodes, with the thick 'southernese' accent, was our bombardier. Bill Frisbee was our radioman. Our crew was completed when a group of five gunners arrived together. Jerry Shenkman, Stan Grosse, Ted

Rossi, Mike McQuade and Bruce Crocker were our shooters, who'd try to keep us alive while we tried to kill Germans.

McGuffey motioned for us to follow him as he headed for a patch of vacant seats. He led off the introductions by standing up. "Frank McGuffey, Paris, Texas. This is my first aircrew, so we'll all be learning the ropes together. I'm the driver." McGuffey sat back down, cueing the next man,

"Horace Hawkins, Muscatine, Iowa, co-pilot," and so it went from person to person, just the bare bones. Some guys brought nicknames with them. 1Lt. Hawkins told us to call him "Hawk," explaining the nickname had been with him since high school because his nose was a real beak.

I introduced myself next and offered my nickname, Red, obviously because of my red hair. I explained I had enlisted after high school and was going to play professional baseball, hopefully for the New York Yankees, after the war.

Bill Frisbee, our radioman from San Bruno, California, had been a fry cook before signing up when he turned 18.

Jim Rhodes opened his mouth, and his lazy drawl betrayed his southern roots. "Anniston, Alabama, is home fer me and Ah am the bombardier. Ah'll be on mah knees a lot, but don't any of you get the wrong a-dea 'bout that. Back home they call me "Dusty," 'cause I guess that goes with roads. Anyways, you fellas can call me Dusty."

Jerry Shenkman was the first of our shooters, our one Jewish crewman from New York City. Proud of his heritage, he suggested we call him "Shenk."

Grosse, Rossi, McQuade and Crocker were our other shooters. McQuade said to call him Mac. Ted Rossi and Stan Grosse hadn't arrived with nicknames, so they were just Ted and Stan until we managed to hang monikers on them.

Bruce Crocker from Gilroy, California, told us to call him '"Croc."

"When I enlisted, the recruiter said that I'd be getting a lot of tail." After a short pause, Croc gave his punch line. "I wonder how he knew I'd be a tail gunner."

"That means I'm in the nose, no problem," said a smiling Jerry Shenkman. "Better to kill Krauts."

With the introductions made, a voice from the auditorium exit called, "Group Six." That was us. McGuffey stood, looking at the speaker. "Let's go." And we followed him from our seats to our waiting escort.

* * * *

Group Six Crew

We stopped next to a taxiway with rows of B-24s parked on either side. Our bunch and two other crews exited the bus. A sergeant spoke to each crew and pointed to a parked plane. "Wait at your aircraft, and your trainers will be along in just a few minutes."

We stood waiting in the Wyoming sun, as Indian summer was still upon us, along with the ever-present background breeze. A convoy of jeeps approached. Each jeep carried four occupants. Two jeeps braked to a stop in front of each crew, and the riders got out.

The men who climbed out were our trainers. They were here to orient us to the logistics of a bomber group. We met Master Sergeant Jones, representing Crew Chiefs. His people — mechanics, radio technicians and sheet metal crews — kept our planes flying. He explained that after each mission, they quizzed each flight crew member about any equipment problems experienced during the flight. If a part needed replacement or a shell hole patched in the 1/8-inch aluminum skin, they made it happen. The four Pratt and Whitney Wasp rotary engines were the crew chief's children, and he handled their care.

A representative from the Quartermaster's corps explained our electrically heated flight suits. Above 10,000 feet, the temperature dropped to minus 50 degrees. Everybody would be cold, since the planes were not heated. Gunners had it the worst. The two waist gunners stood by openable windows on either side of the fuselage. The coldest spot was the nose turret. Wind speed and air seeping in around the turret edges dropped the perceived air temperature even further.

We had classes on the plane's oxygen system. According to our instructor, "At 8,000 feet or above, you need to use oxygen or you'll be disoriented; that is, until it kills you."

Besides not being heated, our planes were not pressurized, so we needed bottled oxygen. Both the oxygen masks and flight suit systems had plug-in connections. Not tangling or disconnecting our own or the next guy's tubes and wires became another concern.

If we wanted them, we were provided with bullet-proof vests, flak jackets and protective helmets. After each mission, our gear went back to the quartermaster for storage, cleaning or repair as needed.

Our five shooters met an armorer. After every mission, his crew removed the .50 caliber Browning machine guns that defended us. Each weapon was cleaned and inspected. Their job was to make sure the eight guns were ready to fire. The armorers reinstalled the guns, then fed belts of bullets into each one. Only the test firings remained for the flight crew to complete once aloft.

We all drew our .45 caliber side-arms before each mission. The servicing and loading of the pistols and their three magazines happened out of our sight.

Next came the fueling crew who'd load each plane with about 2,750 gallons of fuel. Depending on distance to the target, two auxiliary underwing tanks could be added. We had to be away from the plane while it was being fueled, just in case.

After fueling, the camera crews went to work. Three technicians worked to install downward-facing cameras. Pre-loaded with film canisters, the cameras automatically tripped into action when our bombs dropped.

The final trainer to meet with us was the squadron bomb loader. This crew took its orders from the base Operations Officer, after our missions were planned by the Army strategists. The type and size of bombs for the mission came from base ops: high explosive, incendiary, armor piercing, fragmentation or napalm firebombs. Then the planes were loaded with up to 8,000 pounds of bombs. The loaders hoisted the bombs into our bomb bay where they hung suspended by nose and tail shackles. Then they installed two fuses per bomb. The shackles automatically disengaged when the bombardier pressed his bomb release button.

The trainer hit one cautionary note, "just in case," he assured us. "If a bomb shackle doesn't release, the bombardier has to enter the bomb bay and pry the jammed shackle open with a large screwdriver, allowing the bomb to fall." The caution got more than one small gasp or sideways glance and an unknown number of quiet, "Oh, shits."

Our training day complete, we bussed back to the main base and split up. Frank McGuffey told us to meet back for a bus tomorrow morning at 0700. Some of the crew headed back to quarters, others to share a drink at the service club and build our crew identity. I went off to find Fast Eddie.

Eddie was already back at our shared room. As usual, we grabbed our ball gloves and headed for the open space of the drill field. I heard about the composition of his Number Five flight crew, who was who and who did what. Fast Eddie got the same information back about my crew, as the baseball zipped back and forth twenty yards from glove to glove. With our news shared, our heads were temporarily released from the rigors of training. I knew I'd make friends among my crew, but I was glad that I had such a good buddy to share what the army, the war and strangeness of it all demanded. Then we headed back to drop off our gloves and go to dinner.

* * * *

B-24 Liberator Bomber

Our crew was now assembled and had completed its ground-bound introduction to all the specialists supporting every plane. It was time to take our training aloft. For the balance of our three months in Casper, we flew daily. We practiced every activity, no matter how straightforward or seemingly unimportant. Things as simple as moving about while aloft, plugging in our electrically heated suits or oxygen lines. We practiced until each task was part of our muscle memory.

Frank and Horace practiced take-offs and landings. Their ground-bound training now merged with the airborne acts of retracting wheels, closing landing gear doors and the vibrations of flight. Each of us practiced moving to our exit points in case bailing out became necessary.

I learned how to operate in the limited space provided for navigation. Before each flight, our training supervisor gave me that day's route. Then I prepared my map, circling landmarks. Once in the air, finding these landmarks was entirely different from mere pencil lines on a map. The chosen route to the target always included multiple course changes, to confuse the enemy about our actual target.

Our Bombardier practiced kneeling over the Norden bomb site and operating its controls. He also practiced slipping into the bomb bay. Negotiating the eight-inch-wide center board between the stacks of bombs suspended on either side of the bomb bay was tricky. Here he stood once aloft, removing the safety cotter pins from the fuses in the bombs we carried.

Gunners got the feel of their places. Waist gunners stood by windows on either side of the fuselage. The top turret gunner, tail gunner and nose gunner all practiced getting into firing positions and making quick exits to bail out. They also practiced shooting in short bursts, husbanding their supply of bullets.

The Radio operator checked his gear. Could he talk to and receive messages from the ground and other planes? Then he checked that our on-board intercom system worked. During flight, once we passed 8,000 feet, he'd be checking on each crew member every fifteen minutes to make sure no one had passed out from lack of oxygen.

We joked about some of the less glamorous but real-world issues like taking a dump into an empty ammunition box. Our new diet was designed to prevent gas. Not as a courtesy to our fellow crew about the smell of farts. *My own farts of course smelled like roses!* Gas expanding to three times its normal volume when aloft would double us over in pain. That is, if it didn't kill us.

We spent a full day learning how to parachute out of a damaged plane. There were three exits from a crippled B-24. The five gunners had the toughest escape route, out through open bomb bay doors. Every crew member was schooled on his exit route before our first takeoff. No second chances if you got it wrong.

Another day focused on the 'Downed Flyer Survival Kits.' The kit was customized for each crew member. Mine contained six small portrait-style pictures of me wearing European civilian clothes. The pictures were for a fake identity document if we were being aided by one of the underground resistance movements. We got a double-sided page of useful phrases translating from English to French, Danish, Polish or German.

A 'Bail-out Kit' was already clipped to our parachute harnesses. Its 16-pocket vest held rations, medical supplies and survival gear. The kit also had our .45 ACP automatic pistol, waterproof holster and 20 rounds of ammunition. I planned to figure out how to take my ball glove with me.

I learned about the 'relief tube' from bitter experience. The metal tube, our flying urinal, emptied to the outside. At an air temperature of 40 degrees below zero, an accidental contact could cause a painful airborne circumcision or worse.

Once aloft on a mission, the gunners would test fire their guns. Bombardiers would pull the cotter pins from each bomb's fuse, and we would be ready for battle.

Our sojourn in Wyoming over, we headed to Topeka, Kansas, for assignment to a unit and to get our own plane.

9. Topeka, Kansas and Across the Pond, January 1944

8th Air Force, 2nd Combat Bomb Wing, 389th Bomb Group,
567th Squadron,
"The Sky Scorpions"

And there it was, our plane. Her paint job, olive drab above a silver belly, matched our unit assignment. We belonged to the 8th Air Force, 2nd Combat Bomb Wing, 389th Bomb Group, "The Sky Scorpions." Our squadron, the 567th; our logo, a snorting blue-winged dragon with a red bomb in his front talon, all on a yellow background.

The flights to get us across the Atlantic would be flown alone, just us, and I'd never flown over water before. Combined, these two factors turned my blood cold, but I kept my mouth shut about my fears.

Already painted on both sides of our plane was the American white star on a blue circle. A wide orange stripe circled the aircraft's body.

When I asked, "Why the stripe?" I was told "Identification." *What the hell?*

German Heinkel bombers looked like our B-24s at first glance. Twice now, German planes painted to match our bombers had slipped into a returning formation and dropped bombs on an AAC base. The identification stripe was like providing sentries a 'password of the day' to tell friend from foe.

Frank McGuffey found an unexpected detail mounted on his instrument panel: a small brass plate. "Built by Ford Motors, Ypsilanti, Michigan." So, we had the provenance and pedigree of our plane.

Our 567th Squadron was to settle in at AAC Hethel in East Anglia.

Fast Eddie and crew number 5 got their plane too. They were headed for Port Lyautey in French Morocco to fly anti-submarine patrols. His plane's aluminum skin was unpainted, except for the generic AAC stars and its own distinctive tail markings signifying the 480th Anti-submarine group. We would stay in touch as best we could and set one specific meeting; Stockton Joe's Restaurant, July 4th, whenever we both made it home.

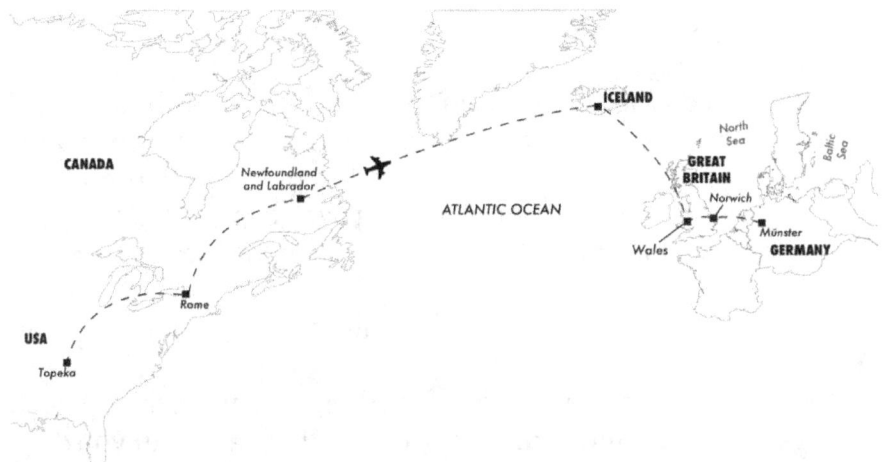

Command dictated our route. We'd fly from Topeka to Rome, New York, then to Newfoundland, Iceland, Wales and finally Norwich in East Anglia. Hethel was our base, just outside Norwich.

Based on experience and caution, our plane took on board two inflatable life rafts and a chemical toilet. The life rafts made absolute sense over the long, cold expanses of the Atlantic. We secured the rafts, neatly folded and tightly packed, near our forward and rear entry hatches in the plane's belly.

The AAC has my everlasting gratitude for the toilet. The ammo box shit shuffle was never fun, private or totally successful. Squatting over an open box, flight suit around your knees, in a bouncing airplane was, well, the shits. With the chemical crapper stashed in the back of the plane, we got a seat. With frame braces to hold if necessary, the air freshness improved.

We flew at 300 miles per hour for five hours to reach the Royal Air Force base in Newfoundland, where we refueled and overnighted. The ride was long, cold, and bumpy. Imagine the joys of trying to drive fast over a rutted dirt road. Everyone had fold-down seats and there was no need for our shooters to be at their guns. So, a card game in the space between the waist guns helped pass the time.

Wheels up at 0800 for our six-hour flight to Iceland. Frank McGuffey kept us below 8,000 feet, so we probably had a few more bumps. In exchange, we weren't on oxygen and the temperature outside the plane stayed a balmy 20 degrees.

Guys dozed when they weren't clustered and gabbing. I tired of seeing only sky as I looked up through the cockpit or water when I glanced down into Dusty Rhodes' plexiglass bomb sight area. I'd pretty near finished my paperback copy of *Riders of the Purple Sage* when Hawk Hawkins turned and woke me from my prairie dreams.

"Red, I've lost the beam. Have you still got our navigation beam in your radio?"

I put my headset on and got nothing. "Hey Frisbee, check your radio. Hawk and I can't hear our radio beam. Can you?"

Bill Frisbee put down his crossword puzzle. "Nothing. I'm checking my equipment."

Hawk and I exchanged looks as we waited for Frisbee's diagnostic check. When it came, it was not good news. "Radio's dead."

I turned back to the cockpit. McGuffey and Hawkins looked down in my direction, perhaps hoping for an answer. I had one more thing we could check. The plexiglass navigation dome, intended for sighting off the stars, could tell us if our radio antenna was in place, damaged or missing.

"Can one of you guys stand up into the nav dome and check the antenna?" I called up above the background noise of engines and wind.

Co-pilot Hawkins contorted around from his seat and stood up in the space behind his usual spot.

"We lost it. No antenna."

Word of the problem made it to the crew. *Well, now I'll get to do what it is they pay me for: navigate,* was the thought that crossed my mind. Hawkins and McGuffey were both looking in my direction. So were Dusty and Frisbee, so I spoke up.

"This is why there is a navigator on board. No worries." To cut the thickening tension, I said, "So, do you still want to go to Iceland?" That brought a smile to our pilot's face. "Stay on this heading, captain, and I'll calculate what you need, and have bearing changes for you in just a minute." And I did.

My backup system was the old-school method the AAC had taught. Known time, speed and distance were calculated and mapped, just in case the radio beam failed.

We made it into Iceland with no more problems, just excitement. Since we had no radio to check in with the Icelandic RAF air controller, three Spitfires came up to meet us. Frank McGuffey came on our intercom as the Spitfires closed in.

"Shooters, keep your waist gun windows closed. Top turret, nose and tail, salute or wave when the Brits come for a look. We don't want to get mistaken for Krauts trying to sneak in."

One fighter stayed in a trailing spot, another above. The third plane pulled alongside, dangerously close to our wing tip, and gave us a look. From behind Hawkins, I saw the gesture for us to follow him down. We did, and survived.

Replacement of our antenna added another day to our sojourn in Reykjavik. Is Iceland always windy or just when I'm there? I planned to return and check it out after the war. During the antenna repair, we made it off base and into town. I can vouch for the local beer and the women. Apparently, being a blonde is legally required. My first love, black-haired Bella Bacigalupo, would be exotic in Iceland.

Wheels up at first light, which here and now wasn't until 0700. As we flew away, the waterfalls and the steam rising from hot spring and geysers were unlike anything I'd ever seen or imagined.

Our last over-water leg, from Iceland to Wales, was the longest, at almost eight hours. Lucky for me, I had found another book, printed in English, at the joint RAF-AAC base in Reykjavik.

Our last leg was from Wales to Norwich in East Anglia. Norwich was the 389th's assembly point. Our 567th Squadron was at AAC Hethel.

10. AAC Hethel, England, February 1944

Home finally at AAC Hethel, our crew was welcomed by our Squadron Commander, Major David Quinn and his Operations Officer, Captain Dan Crandall. Maj. Quinn turned us over to the captain, who gave us the nickel tour of the base.

Our first stop was to our assigned quarters, where we dropped our canvas gear bags. On we went, past the dining hall, showers, latrine and all-ranks service club. Then we began settling into our new home: for how long, nobody knew. I shared a tent with the other officers. Next door to us, the enlisted men in our crew squeezed into another tent.

Most of Hethel base was a sea of olive drab canvas tents. Duck-board wooden sidewalks on the ground connected the different base operations. Headquarters occupied one of the few permanent buildings. Inside HQ, our missions were announced, and I would have my navigators' planning meetings. Across the hall, Dusty Rhodes and the other bombardiers had their own briefings.

We met Technical Sergeant Hartman, the squadron armorer. Next, we visited the Quartermasters' hut, where we'd draw our gear. After that came the briefing tent, radio repair shop, the bomb loaders' shop and our ground crew chief.

MSgt Jack Armstrong considered our plane to be his own and we were mere guests. Each of the four rotary engines became one of his children. His ear would tune to the messages hidden in their hums. Smooth was a happy sound. Any cough, rattle or throb was a cause for concern.

The next morning, Cpt. Crandall caucused with Frank McGuffey outside the mess hall. McGuffey listened and nodded his understanding before turning to us.

"Everybody, take a seat inside. Captain Crandall is going to fill us in on how our missions kick off, so we'll all know what to expect." With that, the ten of us entered and queued up at two vacant tables.

I sat next to Dusty Rhodes. "Dis is when we fine out how da cow et da cabbage in dis yer pasture," quipped Dusty. Co-pilot Horace Hawkins sat down next to Dusty, who nodded, acknowledging his presence. "Whore-ass," the name came out in the thick 'southernese' that passed for Dusty's English.

"Dusty, call me Hawk, Okay?"

All eyes set upon Cpt. Crandall. "Grab a cup of coffee if you want, or a smoke," and he paused, waiting for the new crew's full attention. There were no takers for coffee. Three of our number lit cigarettes and Mac McCabe fired up his briar pipe. "You have had the best training the Air Corps could provide. You represent an investment of considerable time and money. I'm going to lay out our operational procedures.

"As the 8th Air Force learned hard lessons, our tactics evolved. Chief among the lessons learned is using mass formation flying to maximize the protective value of every machine gun. Think of it, 100 planes equal 800 machine guns all working together for mutual protection."

He paused. "In like manner, our enemy has evolved their anti-aircraft defenses into box patterns we have to fly into and out of on every mission."

At the thought of having to fly through two sides of an anti-aircraft box, some of us exchanged glances, while others sucked harder on their cigarettes.

"Pilots," Frank and Hawk's attention sharpened at his words. "Arrange to check the briefing board located inside the main briefing room. You already have your air crew numbers. The board will list on-deck crews by number. The numbers are posted twelve hours in advance of mission wheels-up times."

"Ground crews get awakened three hours before flight crews. Your crew chief and his assistant will pre-flight each plane and then the planes are fueled and loaded. Each engine is started and revved up to flight speed." He stopped, giving us time to digest the new information.

"Questions so far?" When no one spoke up, Crandall continued, his eyes moving slowly from one face to another.

"The Squadron chaplains will join you in the mess hall for your pre-flight meal. After breakfast, all flight crews meet for their main briefings. Primary and secondary targets are revealed. You'll hear a weather report. The Intelligence office will brief you on what they know about enemy anti-aircraft defenses, both guns and fighters protecting the target. You'll be told about safe emergency landing zones." And again, the captain paused to check for questions. To a man, we remained silent.

"The main briefing continues, providing a timeline for each squadron's departure. The strategy is to employ multiple squadrons from different bases. The morning sky can be crowded with planes. So, following the time and altitude of your in-flight rendezvous is crucial for our own safety," and he paused again.

"The main briefing concludes with us synchronizing our watches. The navigators, radio operators and bombardiers now go to a second briefing." Dusty Rhodes, Bill Frisbee and I concentrated our attention, as things focused on our jobs.

"Navigators, you'll get detailed information for map plotting. Note installations on your maps, so you know when and where to dump the bags of radar-confusing chaff. Mark escape routes in case you can't make it back to base.

"Radio operators, you'll receive the assigned frequencies for the radio beam navigation." McGuffey, Frisbee and I shared glances and we each gave subtle signals showing our understanding. Cpt. Crandall made another pause and checked the ten faces, confirming that none of his audience had visibly tuned out.

"When everyone's briefing ends, you'll hit the quartermaster's hut for your flight equipment. They issue your heated flight suit. Pick up your parachute and small 'escape kit' that has been customized to your flight path. There will be maps, a phrase card and money specific to the flight path. Anyone who wants can add a flak apron and protective helmet. Your .45 caliber pistols and their magazines will be returned to you after cleaning, checking and loading by the armorers. Finally, fully briefed and equipped, you get one last opportunity to visit the latrine and then your crew will be bussed to the waiting plane."

Cpt. Crandall now made the rounds, shaking the hand of each of us and intoning, "Godspeed."

* * * *

Frank McGuffey gathered us all together after the briefing. "Fellas, here are my directions for us all. I get my marching orders from up the chain of command. I'll have some advance notice on missions. How much, I don't know. So, I need everybody to keep me informed about anything that might take you out of our squadron area. Be prepared to fly every morning by zero six hundred. I'll share what I know. If you have a pass to town or are going on sick call, make sure that you tell Hawk or myself.

"You'll know what I know as soon as I know. Flight officers will verify that everyone is informed." Pausing for a moment, Frank lit another cigarette. "Questions?" Nobody spoke up.

We had no questions because he had no answers. We'd all have to wait and wonder. There was no answer to be had until Frank got the word. Then we'd know.

* * * *

Dusty Rhodes had seen my baseball glove propped up on my bunk in our four-man tent. "Hey Red, Ah played ball back in Anniston. How 'bout y'all and me toss dat ol' whores hide around?" It took me a minute to decipher Dusty's southernese. My eyes lit up when he assumed a batter's stance and pantomimed swinging a bat. Then I understood — baseball!

"Heck, yes," my response no longer delayed. "What did you play?"

"Oudfield" Dusty had tossed me a life preserver. The cold, damp and perpetually gray skies of February in England had me in a funk.

Hethel had its own background symphony of sounds. The ever-present odor of aviation fuel and the drone of engines might have slipped from my consciousness, except for the periodic sirens. The siren's scream meant a shot-up plane or one with wounded aboard was coming in.

The siren's wail made it impossible for me to step away from the war for even a second. Some guys used alcohol; others found comfort by making a deep dive into their faith. Non-stop card games abounded, but I'd yet to find my escape until Dusty saw my ball glove.

"Do you have a glove?" I asked. I picked up my glove from the bunk and showed my friend the ball concealed in the pocket.

"Yup, Ah sho do. Ah kep 'er earled up, case I get a call from da bigs." My ear was becoming more tuned to Alabama English. "Owl go getter," and he did.

I ducked my head out of our tent. Sun threatened to break through the perpetual gray. With our gloves in hand, we stepped outside, found some open space and began our pitch and catch. As our arms loosened and muscle memory returned, we lengthened our distance, but stayed within a conversation range.

Dusty Rhodes had a hell of an arm, as I found out when his throw stung my hand. I'd have to pay attention to catching his tosses in the glove's webbing and not the pocket. "So which team you gonna play for?" I asked.

"The Nu Yaurk Giants, man. They god a farm team in Anniston," he drawled. "N' you?"

"The Yankees. I'm going to be their shortstop after Frankie Crosetti retires. If I make it back OK."

"She-it, we gonna make it back an ta the bigs, man! Cept yu wool only play me 'n the Wrld Series."

* * * *

At mail call later that day, I got my first letter from Fast Eddie.

> *Hi, Red!*
> *You've got the same censor rules that I'm living with, so I won't write anything that would only be crossed out. I arrived safe on station. We named our bird "Tiburon"– shark in Spanish. Our bird is new from its nest in Texas instead of Michigan like yours. Fishing has been good and our driver, Haywood Van Husen, has picked up some tricks, so the big fish don't even feel it when we set the hook. My folks are fine. I hope yours are the same. I'm keeping my glove oiled up, and you do the same.*
> *Eddie.*

* * * *

The squadron gave us two weeks of practice before flying our first mission. In all our radio traffic, Hethel was 'Station 114,' so as not to help the Germans make a counterstrike. In hindsight, those precious training days before we headed across the channel and into harm's way were critical to our staying alive.

Here's the deal. Our squadron had 12 planes and there were four squadrons stationed at Hethel. We were one of 19 AAC airfields in East Anglia. You do the math.

For every mission, each field had its assigned launch time to a designated rendezvous point 8,000 feet up over the English Channel. Twenty-four heavy bomber groups vectoring in from different paths made for a crowded patch of sky. Command sent up brightly striped, red-white-blue B-24s as flying signposts. These 'assembly planes' told us, by radio, where to fly in the aerial assembly racetrack oval, until all groups had arrived.

Pilots knew their places in the launch queue. We waited, our four engines idling, until we got the green light from the flight controller. We lifted off and headed to our assembly point in the sky. Entire flights circled the rendezvous spot, waiting for all of our attack squadrons to arrive.

Our congested sky sometimes got even more crowded when the Royal Air Force squadrons returned to base after their night bombing missions. Often these aerial crossings to and from Europe were the most dangerous part of our mission.

Eventually our bombers assembled into one tight mass of planes bristling with machine guns. Then those beautiful sheepdogs, our P-51 Mustang fighters, appeared on our flanks. God bless the fighters!

When we crossed the Atlantic en route to England we flew with the jet stream at our backs, speeding us on our way. This was not to be the case over Europe, we were warned. These newly discovered global winds between 12,000 and 20,000 feet, where we'd be flying, would work against us as often as for us.

* * * *

February 20, 1944 was "Big Week," a series of 1,000-plane raids targeting the German aircraft industry. It was common knowledge that the long-awaited invasion of Hitler's "Fortress Europe" would happen soon.

Word came down to crew level on the 19th. Frank McGuffey told us to meet at our usual corner of the mess tent at noon.

"Guys, we finally get to do what we've been waiting for. We take off at 0500 tomorrow. We're going to Germany. That means an early morning for us all. Rendezvous back here at 0300, ready to go." He stopped to light a cigarette and give us time to take it all in. Extinguishing the match, he checked our faces. "Questions, anyone?"

"Where are we going, Cap?" asked Mac McQuade, our top turret gunner. The officers already knew, as our second briefings had disclosed all the details of our route, target and the expected German defense posture. Only our five shooters didn't know.

"Muenster. We're going to hit an aircraft production plant," explained our pilot. "Get a good night's rest, guys. Tomorrow is the real deal," and our full crew briefing ended.

* * * *

The next morning our four flying officers exited our tent together and took the three-block walk on the wooden sidewalk to our squadron mess hall. Our five shooters were already there. Some of us ate, but nobody drank over one cup or glass. My painful experience had imprinted on us all the logistics of taking a leak while wearing a heated flight suit. At 0330, after a Protestant chaplin had stopped by, Frank signaled it was time for us to gear up.

It was two walkway lengths to our squadron quartermaster where we all geared up. Parachutes, side-arms, flight suits and our custom downed-airman kits went out to each man. All five of our gunners also took metal helmets and vests. Frank McGuffey checked with each of us. "Got what you need?" he asked. Each acknowledgment got a pat on the shoulder or back slap. Seeing us all ready, he led us outside to a waiting bus.

It was 0415 when the bus pulled up to our plane. Frank told us to wait until he checked if our fueling was done. As we waited, the bomb loaders finished their work. I recognized 500- and 1,000-pound bombs going aboard. Their paint identified them as high explosive or fragmentation munitions. The last items loaded before the bomb bay doors closed were 100-pound napalm firebombs, three to a shackle.

McGuffey found we were gassed and ready to go. "OK guys, time to load up." We entered through the front and rear floor hatches. Everyone made their way to their spots and plugged in the flight suit's heat cable. Hanging up where we'd left them were our oxygen masks. I attached the oxygen line to my mask in anticipation of donning it when we hit 8,000 feet.

Our crew chief had already warmed up the engines, and once the hatches and the waist windows were closed, they each kicked over on the first try. The 1900-horsepower Pratt & Whitneys settled into a comforting familiar hum. It was now 0500.

McGuffey knew our place in the launch queue: number 6 of 12. He increased power and taxied the plane from our hard site out onto a taxiway, where we fell in line some 100 feet behind the number 5 plane. Our three sister squadrons at Hethel would follow us into the sky.

We waited, our engines idling, for the green light from the flight controller. Frank held us straight on the runway as our engines came up to full power. At the green light, he released the brakes and down the runway we rolled, gaining speed along the 3,000 ft. cement path. We lifted off, banked left and headed to our assembly point in the sky.

Over the English Channel our gunners test-fired their guns. This had to be done while our squadrons were still alone. When the armada formed, it became harder to avoid hitting a friendly target by accident.

After meeting the assembly plane, we'd circle at our rendezvous point until all 48 aircraft were in formation. Then we'd head for our meeting point with 20 other formations in a 1,000-plane armada and begin our deadly work.

Bill Frisbee confirmed we had a clear signal for radio beam navigation. Then he confirmed with the pilot and with me that we also had the beam through our headsets. Next Frisbee checked that each crew member's intercom worked.

Dusty Rhodes unclipped from his parachute harness and headed down under the wings into the depths of the bomb bay. He got jolted from side to side as he climbed onto the four hanging rows of bombs to remove the pins from those suspended above. He pulled cotter pins from the 500- and 1,000-pound bomb fuses. Now the bombs were armed. Strapped into my fold-down seat, I felt every air pocket as the plane no longer rode smoothly. To me, a giant hand slapped at the plane, bumping us, rattling us and keeping everyone ready to grab a convenient handhold.

Once assembled, our 1,000 planes climbed from 8,000 to 20,000 feet. Our flight time to Muenster, in the northwest of Germany, just over 100 miles from the Netherlands border, was about four hours.

I knew from our briefing to expect the first land fighters about 40 minutes out from the target. Both arrived as predicted.

We all knew what was coming, but the knowing and the living through were two different things. German fighters arrived first. Our formation didn't change as these metal sharks sped above, below and through our formation. Our strength was in the massed firepower of our thousands of .50 caliber guns, so no one broke formation. From my station behind and below the cockpit I could only see above Hawk Hawkins' shoulders. I chose not to stick my head up into the plexiglass navigation dome.

The simultaneous rattles of eight thousand guns mixed with the roar of what seemed like hundreds of Messerschmitt 109 and Focke-Wulf 190 engines. Our P-51 long-range fighters added the whine of their engines and the rattle of their guns to the frightful roar of battle. True to their mission, our P-51s never left our formation to go chasing enemy planes.

Then the flak started. The Germans had their 88- and 105-millimeter anti-aircraft guns arrayed in a box formation around Muenster. Their shells were pre-set to explode at a certain altitude.

The explosions rocked our plane. The sky above our cockpit was now black with overlapping bursts that sent halos of steel flying in all directions. Suddenly we lurched and lurched again. The combined roar of gunfire and planes concealed the sound of metal daggers piercing our thin aluminum skin.

"Anybody hurt back there?" came the question from the cockpit. Shooters too busy to key their microphones were slow in responding.

"Tan minutes to tar-get Cap'n," Dusty's words went out to everyone's headset. "Bomb durs open." With my senses overloaded by noise within and without, and the lurching from exploding shells, we passed into the eye of the storm and the anti-aircraft fire stopped. Outside, the 109s and 190s still nipped at our planes, but the hell of gunfire had subsided.

"Steady on Cap'n; 10 seconds ta drap." I counted down the seconds in my mind. Dusty's radio squawked that the lead plane had dropped its bombs. "Bombs awa-hay," and Dusty released our deadly cargo. The sound of the lead plane's bombs now reached our ears. A continual string of overlapping explosions continued as each wave of bombs struck the target.

Perhaps only in my head, but there in the middle of so much chaos, it was silent for a moment. I realized my eyes were wet and my mouth dry. My breathing began to settle back to normal.

"Bomb durs keylosd." I could feel our plane, now 8,000 pounds lighter, join the armada in a steep bank to the left and back toward the coast.

"Damage report: anybody hurt?" Frank's voice sounded in our ears during the relative calm. No one had been hit. Stan Rossi informed us the Germans had punched a few holes in our skin.

"Hang on guys, round two coming up," and again the sky bloomed black with explosions and clouds of steel daggers hurled our way. What was actually about three minutes seemed hours as each second brought more fury, but finally, we exited the reach of the German guns.

When the coastline appeared somewhere East of Bremerhaven, the German fighters broke off for home. The intercom was silent for many miles as each of us replayed the hell we'd just passed through. The silence lasted until the coast of England appeared and our voices returned.

Frank set us down and taxied off to the first available hard stand. Our crew chief and four of his team opened our bottom hatches as soon as the propellers had stopped spinning.

"Any wounded?" was his first question.

Thankfully, "No."

His team helped each of the crew climb down and out of the plane. As I stood waiting for a bus to take us for our debriefing, I surveyed the plane. I counted 30 punctures to our metal skin.

One shell had slashed into us below my seat. I made a mental note to check out an armored plate to sit on when the Quartermaster issued gear. I did not kneel and kiss the tarmac, but I wanted to.

Fifty planes didn't make it back. Thankfully, the 567th was spared. Two of our sister squadrons had twenty fewer men that night. Today, the war had become real.

11. Back in the Lion's Den, February 1944

"Once more into the breach, dear friends, once more;"
William Shakespeare

If you have never seen the ocean, my words, any words, cannot describe its sounds, smells and boundless size. So it was for me when our enemy began actively trying to kill me. Playing catch with Dusty Rhodes or in the never-ending pinochle game in our tent, nobody talked about our chances of being killed. All of us thought about death, but no one ever spoke about it.

I saw an article in Life Magazine which must have missed our ever-present military censors. It said that our 8th Air Force bomber crews were more likely to die in action than a Marine storming a beach. Sobering stuff. So why did we keep climbing aboard our plane and flying into harm's way? For me, it was 10 percent not wanting to get court-marshalled. 30 percent was not wanting to disappoint my parents. And 60 percent was because I couldn't let down the guys who were up there with me.

On February 25, the last day of Big Week, we went back to Muenster and flew into the same hell we'd escaped before. Knowing what to expect didn't make it any easier. This trip I checked out a ballistic plate to sit on, so I wouldn't get my balls blown off. All the sheet metal holes had been patched and our olive-green upper body paint was now mottled by the touched-up spots.

I remembered guidance from the previous briefing, "If you go down in Germany, try to make it to the coast. Look for a ship flying the Swedish flag and try to stow away on board." Now I paid more attention to anything that suggested the safest route to the coast.

This time, the Germans knew we were coming and welcomed us with a sky full of anti-aircraft shells that bloomed into hundreds of metal daggers. Their puffs of black smoke looked to me like flower petals. German fighter planes had changed their attack plans. Now, besides nipping at the edges of our armada, they dove through our formations, shooting as they came. With steep angles of attack, only our P-51s from above and our top turrets from below got off shots at them.

From behind Hawk Hawkins' seat in the cockpit, I saw more of the action than from the navigator's table. I watched as some poor bastard had his left wing sheared off by collision with a diving Messerschmitt. Both planes spun down, out of control, to their deaths. *I hope it's over quick*, was my only thought as hunter and prey dropped from sight.

We shuddered but kept flying when ground fire took a chunk out of one of our tail fins. Crock, our tail gunner, had shrapnel slice through his calf, just before we passed inside the German anti-aircraft box. Still hounded by their fighters, this was as calm as things would get until we were over the English Channel again.

Bill Frisbee was the only crew member able to help. Unclipping his parachute, heater and oxygen hoses, Bill made his way to the back. A blast of wind struck the plane as he moved. Its impact slammed him into an airframe brace. Hand over hand he continued to the back. The Croc was still shooting as Bill sprinkled sulfa powder into the cut flight suit. The suit had to stay on, or Crocker would probably freeze, so Frisbee bound the calf wound as tightly as possible from outside the suit.

"Croc, I gotta get back to the radio before I pass out from lack of oxygen. Can you make it for a while longer?"

Still scanning for targets, the Croc nodded.

We made it out of the box after delivering our bomb load. Frank McGuffey banked hard left and headed for the coast. Dusty and I helped pull our wounded tail gunner out of the far back. We laid him down on a section of our interior floor deck. Frisbee radioed ahead that we had a wounded man on board. Lighter now, once the bombs were dropped, we made it back to Hethel in two hours.

An ambulance was outside as soon as our props stopped spinning. The Croc needed only six stitches to close the wound to the meat of his calf. He flew again in ten days.

But one hundred and two of our planes didn't make it back, including three planes from Hethel. There were over a thousand empty beds that night.

Jack Hathaway didn't return to their ground spot, two planes down the row from us, but a month later, we got the good news that he and his crew had made it to Sweden and were interned at a resort town in the mountains.

* * * *

With Big Week over, we enjoyed some downtime. Between March and May 1944, we flew to Merseburg and targeted an oil refinery. At Sangerhausen we hit a rail yard. Raids on Friedrichshafen, Politz and Pforzhem filled our aerial dance card. We never came back without battle damage. If not shrapnel wounds to our aluminum skin, there were always bullet holes from the German fighters, it seemed.

Dusty Rhodes and I gained a bat. Unfortunately, all we could put our hands on was one for cricket. "This durn theng ain't no good fur baseball," he concluded. Try as he might, the shape of a cricket bat sent every other ball careening off hard left or right. It was better than nothing, and for knocking grounders about our improvised infield, it did the job. In a letter home, I'd asked if Dad could send me a ball bat. Four other guys, seeing us pitch and catch, joined our group. Heck, we might put together a team!

A stranger watched as we did our best to be an infield. Everyone playing was dressed in mechanic's jump suits or work-a-day utilities. The silent stranger always dressed in khaki, and emblems of rank sparkled on his collar. He was a full-bird colonel. Finally, Dusty and I decided it was time to invite him over and into our game if he wanted.

"You and the big fella are pretty good," the stranger observed as I walked over to him from where I'd been at shortstop.

"Sir, would you like to join us? You are welcome," and I saluted his rank, one notch below a General Officer. His face seemed familiar, but I couldn't yet connect it to a briefing or even a drink at the Officers' Club.

His smile broadened at the invitation, and he extended a hand to me. "I'm Jimmy. I'm a pilot here with the 565th. How about we skip saluting out here on the ball field?"

"Yes, sir." I returned his smile.

"Let's skip the 'sir.' Here I'm just plain Jimmy, fair enough?"

"Come on, Jimmy, let me introduce you to the rest of the guys." I motioned for my five friends to come over and meet our new prospective player. I stood beside Dusty, who'd been playing catcher, since we didn't have room for an outfield to put him in. We didn't have a ball diamond, let alone an outfield. The four guys trotted in and grouped around Jimmy.

"Guys, this is Colonel Jimmy. He's a pilot. But here on the ball field he's just Jimmy." We took turns shaking hands and briefly introducing ourselves. Dusty leaned over and with a half-turn of his head, spoke. "Dat ole boy looks familyar."

Jimmy had reached down and picked up the cricket bat from where it lay on our improvised home plate. "Looks like you fellas could use a real baseball bat. I'll have to look into that. I'll see what I can do. I'll find myself a glove, but for now, can I borrow one from whoever's at bat?"

It worked out fine. When our practice had to end, I told Colonel Jimmy to check for us here, whenever any of us had free time.

"I fly whenever I can, fella. I love being in the air, but I'll see you all back here first chance I get," said Jimmy. A smile never left his face, which I had yet to place, as we parted.

A shooter from Bob Evan's crew bumped me on the shoulder. "Do you know who that is?"

I shook my head "No."

"That's Jimmy Stewart, the movie actor."

Three weeks later, a baseball bat in hand, Stewart found us at our usual spot. He waved hello and then passed the bat over. "See if this works for you, Dusty."

Rhodes examined the bat, tapping its grip down on the ground to check there were no cracks. As he did, he looked at a round paper tag, thumb-tacked to the business end of the bat. "Cooper" was all it read.

Jimmy watched as Rhodes and I fixed our gazes on the tag. It was a movie prop. "The Pride of the Yankees." The bat passed from hand to hand. Everybody wanted to put their hands where Gary Cooper had held the bat. Finally, Jimmy broke the spell of the moment. "Come on now, let's play some ball."

And we did.

12. D-Day, June 6, 1944

They had us up at 0300. We knew the first troops would hit the beach at 0630 and surprise was our best weapon and biggest hope. The Germans had 55 divisions in France. They could hurl our guys back into the sea if they brought their 10-to-1 numerical superiority to bear. Our job was to stop German reinforcements.

The Brits started dumping 5,000 tons of bombs on the German coast defenses on the night of June 5th. Their bombing also worked as a distraction. Just before midnight on June 5th we began landing 1200 gliders carrying shock troops and supplies. Then 18,000 airborne troops from the 82nd, the 101st Airborne Division and the British 6th Airborne Division dropped behind the invasion beaches. For the first time since Dunkirk, Allied soldiers were on the ground in Northern Europe.

We'd bomb the coast and a 40-mile half-circle inland, just behind our airborne troops, with every plane able to fly. Our job was to destroy the roads, rail lines and bridges needed to channel German Panzers to the coast. Our bombs would hit the ground starting at 0530, first light on June 6, 1944. With our bomb bays loaded and gas tanks full, the short flight time allowed us to hit and rearm, hit and rearm, at a ferocious pace. We'd be flying without our sheepdogs, the P-51s. They would be busy strafing targets of opportunity on the ground.

Since Big Week in February, the Germans hadn't been able to replace their losses in experienced fighter pilots. Trainees flew more and more of our enemy's planes. The Germans pulled back fighters from France and Holland, consolidating their units for home defense. Their best pilots were being saved. They'd fly the soon-to-come Messerschmitt 262 jet fighter. Air Marshal Hermann Goering told Adolph Hitler that this super plane would turn the tide of air superiority back in favor of the Reich.

* * * *

At 0530, our lead plane was over the French coast and so was a thick blanket of clouds. Our formation circled in a holding position over the channel, as wave after wave of bombers got the word that clouds prevented our bombing. Other formations from different bases had their take-offs delayed. With our gas tanks full, our four Hethel squadrons could hold in an aerial racetrack path for up to seven hours.

At 0930, Bill Frisbee passed the word that the coast was clear enough to bomb, and they ordered us in. Our target was a single map grid square. Each of our squadrons targeted a different bridge, road or railroad line in our square. For the first time, I was to be a true navigator, as each plane's bombardier dialed in the Norden cross hairs and dropped his bombs at his own time.

The deadly German coast defenses were sighted toward the beaches and not the air. We got shot at from the ground, but the black blooms of anti-aircraft flowers were nothing compared to our missions over Germany. The 389th flew every flight-worthy plane in all our squadrons every day between the 6th and 10th of June, making over 14,000 sorties. With every target in a grid square destroyed, we moved to a new hunting ground. Somewhere during these five days I realized that I'd stopped flinching at the bumps and bursts we all experienced.

The damage and death that we were visiting on French cities, towns and villages were not lost on any of us. On June 14, we bombed Le Havre to suppress the German E-boats. These fast attack boats were hectoring our landing forces and the constant stream of supplies flowing from England to the French coast.

In the early hours of July 7, we began bombing to support the Saint-Lo breakout. Our guys on the ground were bogged down in the hedgerow countryside. We needed to break the German grip as we moved to capture the strategic port of Cherbourg. Our troops were still being supported through the artificial Mulberry harbors we'd created off the Normandy coast. Supplying our forces with everything from gas to grub was key, and we needed a real port to support our people.

* * * *

On July 11th, the 567th was part of a raid on the rail marshaling yards outside Munich. German trains moved much more than supplies to the front and wounded to the rear. We were told that the trains assembled at Munich moved stolen loot from all over Europe back into Germany. Trains from Munich also moved thousands of Jews, gypsies, and other victims to death camps in Germany and Poland. Squadrons from another bomb group were going to bomb a Munich airfield.

Two of our four squadrons lifted off at 08:30. We were all loaded with 2,000-pound high explosive bombs. These 14-foot-long behemoths were the largest explosives we ever carried. They would crater the yard and put it out of action for a good while.

German fighters were few, but flak from their anti-aircraft was heavy. As we entered the anti-aircraft box, they hit two of us. I saw our number 10 plane feather its left outboard engine.

The other plane bore the 564th Sq. tail color markings. Its left wing had visible damage, making it hard to fly and problematic to land. Both planes would try to make it to neutral Switzerland. They headed off under the protection of three friendly fighters.

The attack leader then designated Dusty Rhodes lead bombardier for our formation. Planes would drop their bombs on his call. I saw Dusty kneeling over the Norden, above the plexiglass window in the plane's nose. Dusty, Frisbee our radioman, and Frank McGuffey were in constant intercom communication.

"T-ewe minutes to tar-get, Cap'n," Dusty's words went out to everyone's headset. "Bomb durs open." This was Dusty's show, and I was just a passenger at the moment.

"Steady Cap'n, ten sek-ants to drap."

As usual, I counted down the seconds in my mind.

"Bombs away," and Dusty released our deadly cargo. Frisbee radioed. "Drop-drop-drop" and all our planes let loose their bombs. Above the roar of our engines, a string of explosions from below signaled we could turn for home.

But what was I not hearing? One minute…two minutes and still I didn't hear Dusty's words, "Bomb durs keylosed." What I did hear was the whine of electric motors cycling on and off below me in the bomb bay. Farther from the bay, Frank and Hawk were perhaps too far to hear but not too far to not care. Those three magic words, "Bomb doors closed," were their keys to our making a fast escape from the hostile air of southern Bavaria. I was the first to ask. "Dusty, is everything alright?"

"I'm gonna get back thar and luk," came his response through the intercom speaker built into my soft flight helmet. "Hole tight, I'm on ma way." Dusty made his way back from the nose to the navigator's station. There, a two-foot by two-foot door just behind my seat led from the flight deck to the bomb bay.

I knew my friend would have had to disconnect his oxygen hose to leave his station. Even with Munich having been a lower-risk bombing run, we were still above 8,000 feet. When his head appeared in the passageway, I grabbed his shoulder to help him stand and passed him my oxygen mask. I'd manage for a few minutes without it. With the mask on, his eyes dilated as he sucked in sweet breaths of bottled oxygen.

"Ah thank one of the bomb dur chains com offa the gear wheel," said Dusty. He'd been briefed about such an occurrence and knew the simple fix to get things back on track. The door assemblies always looked to me like the roll top of my dad's desk, only made of metal. I passed my oxygen mask back to his hand.

Dusty's eyes closed as he breathed in long pulls of oxygen before passing the mask back to me and opening the access door. The wind noise inside the plane rose. I felt cabin air being sucked down and out through the door by our 300-mile-per-hour airspeed. He disappeared down the access door into the bomb bay. Through the door opening, I saw only a sea of blue, speckled with cotton-white clouds.

Above me, I caught bits of the conversation from the cockpit. We weren't picking up speed as Frank and Hawk expected our plane to, once lightened by 8,000 pounds of bomb and 40 percent of our fuel load. The two pilots were checking and rechecking engine performance. Each of our 1,900 horsepower engines seemed to be performing beautifully, but here it was: a mystery.

Dusty's head emerged as he climbed the ladder out of the bomb bay. He pointed to my mask and pantomimed putting the mask over his uncovered face. I passed it over and shut the trap door once his knees we solidly on the floor. He sucked in air and handed the mask back to me, then keyed his intercom microphone.

"Capn, soon as y'all kin, take er down ta 7,000. Kin ya come down? I'm here with Red."

Dusty and I shared my mask, back and forth. We both felt our descent and soon there was enough air that the masks weren't needed. He motioned a two-finger come hither gesture so I could hear him above the combined roar of engines and air stream.

"We gut five foot of bomb hangin' down outside the bomb bay like a giant metal dong tween yur legs. We can't land with dat thang a-hanging." His tone and his fixed unblinking gaze were all business; no panic here, but deadly serious, as dead we all might soon be. Leaning in close again, he added more.

"If dat thang takes a hit, it'll go off," and he paused and blinked before going on. "It'll be ova quick." And he leaned back, resting on his knees and heels, as Frank came through the opening between the cockpit and my deck.

I sat back into my seat and folded down the auxiliary seat behind my station that waist gunner Ted Rossi occupied during takeoff and landing. Frank took the seat and Dusty leaned in, repeating for the pilot what he'd seen in the bomb bay beneath our feet. The news he got was all bad and Frank paused the briefing to key his mic.

"Hawk, circle in place, tight as you can. Don't leave the box until I say." Hawk Hawkins made no vocal response to an order that was unheard of. Instead, he turned half around in his seat and leaned down toward the three of us. He took off his mask and mouthed one word, "why?" Hawk got no answer from any of us, but our silent, upturned faces must have said volumes. He turned back to the controls.

With our heads close as the three balls of a pawn shop sign came Frank's question for Dusty. "What can we do? We can't land. A flak hit blows us out of the sky. Bailing out over Germany doesn't look good," and he stopped. His eyes never left Dusty. "Other choices?" When no answer came from either of us, Frank spoke again. "My plane, my problem. I want to look." He rose from the thin padding of the folding seat, but Dusty put out his hand, palm open, stopping his rise and speaking. "Mah bomb, mah problem."

The bombardier moved quickly, first to an inflight tool kit to take out a large screwdriver. Then, moving back to the access hatch, he descended onto the eight-inch catwalk that crossed the bay. Frank moved past the opening to Frisbee's radio position. I moved from my seat to lie flat on the deck, my head and one arm down into the maelstrom of roaring air and engines. The constant bumping of the winds shook our plane. Behind my back, I heard Frank telling Frisbee to tell the rest of our flight that we were staying and to go on without us.

Looking down from my perch, I saw the green metal of the giant bomb hanging down through the open bay doors. Dusty Rhodes stood on the catwalk, screwdriver in one hand, his other holding on to an exposed airframe brace supporting his catwalk perch. All of his strength from one arm wasn't budging the jaws of the shackle.

Turning more to his task meant giving up his hold on the airframe. I could see that only the hanging bomb in front of him and the eight inches of catwalk under his feet kept him from falling to his death. With the screwdriver held in a two-hand grip, the big man slammed upward, forcing the welded bomb attachment lug down onto the shackle jaws. Again, he slammed his only tool against the lug, and still no luck.

A sudden gust twisted Dusty and slammed his hip into the airframe brace. He hugged the bomb with one arm to keep from falling into the empty sky below. The 18-inch cylinder that might kill us was stopping his fall. My mind was empty, but my senses full from the roars inside and outside the open trap door. I watched as Dusty tried a new tack, now wedging the screwdriver blade between the side of the shackle and bomb lug. Now he could push with both arms and all the combined strength of his back and legs. With one mighty shove, he slammed the blade forward against the jaw of the shackle. Suddenly, the bomb released. With only open air in front and behind himself, Dusty dropped the screwdriver and grabbed the airframe brace. He hugged it as we bounced in the sudden turbulence.

I rolled sideways and, keying my intercom, yelled above the roar of the wind. "He did it. It's gone! Get us out of here," and away we went. Rolling back to the open hatch, I heard before I saw. Dusty had reached the auxiliary bomb bay door control button. The roller doors were closing.

As the doors closed, the sound and rush of air both diminished. Dusty slowly made his way to the bottom of the six-foot ladder that led up and out of the bomb bay. Too tired to climb the few steps, he hugged the ladder tight to his chest. I just waited above, my one arm held down, my hand open to help my friend.

I called to Frisbee, "Bill, come help me." Now two arms hung down above the ladder rungs and we grabbed the wrists of our bombardier. As we got him out of the lower bay, I motioned to Bill and said, "Over here." We sat Dusty in the fold-down seat by my station. I moved his arm through the seat's shoulder straps and buckled him in just before his head sagged forward and his eyes closed. With Frisbee beside me, I placed my oxygen mask over Dusty's face. Bill and I would share his mask for the moment, so Dusty could revive.

I stepped up to the flight deck behind Hawk Hawkins' seat. I patted both pilots on their shoulders. "Let's get the hell out of here." Frank signaled with a thumbs-up and the Hawk vigorously nodded his head. Looking out through the cockpit windows, I saw a lone P-51 had stayed to fly a protective over-watch, even at this greater peril. *God bless Dusty and God bless our sheepdogs.*

P-51 Mustang Fighter

We passed through the gauntlet of ground fire undamaged. With our own P-51 still giving us protective cover, we flew out of Germany. Frank, Hawk and I together in the cockpit agreed, "We owe that P-51 driver a drink."

Once over the channel, Frank radioed to base, describing how Dusty Rhodes had saved our plane and our lives. There on the tarmac when we landed, a row of jeeps waited. They followed us back to our hard stand.

We exited through front and rear access doors with a revived Dusty. When he first tried to stand, he collapsed back into the seat. With nothing to grab for support, he spoke up. "Kin you fellers give me a hand up an' outah this gull-durn plane. Ma hip gut banged up sumthin' afull."

With two of us below and two above we got our friend up, out and to the ground.

Outside, as a welcoming committee, were Squadron Commander Quinn and all the other pilots and bombardiers from our squadron. Frank McGuffey was last through the front exit hatch and, realizing who was waiting, he called us to attention.

Major Quinn returned our salutes and called us to stand "at ease." Cpt. Crandall passed him a box and pointed to Dusty. The Major carried the box under one arm like he was packing a football. He strode over to our ranks, stopped in front of Rhodes, and saluted our bombardier. "Second Lieutenant Rhodes," he said.

Dusty returned the salute.

Major Quinn extended the box and held out his other hand, giving Rhodes a congratulatory shake. "You are one brave son-of-a-bitch and a credit to Alabama."

Dusty snuck a glance at the box — Jack Daniels whisky — and smiled. "Tank ya sur." I saw that all the pilots and bombardiers, including Col. Jimmy Stewart, were now saluting Dusty. As Major Quinn walked away, over his shoulder we heard, "Dismissed."

Unable to fly, Dusty was grounded by the squadron Flight Surgeon until further notice. Three months later, at an all-squadron formation, we all saluted Dusty as he received the Distinguished Flying Cross from 389th Bomb Group Commanding Officer, Col. Robert Miller.

13. Catching Our Breath

Frank McGuffey kept a blackboard above his bunk in our tent. The board listed our crew by name with a note showing our status: clear, on leave, hospital, etc. Opposite Dusty's name he chalked "OSO," AAC shorthand for "out screwing off."

They cleared him to fly after three weeks of rest, but during his absence, we flew with a newly arrived replacement, Elmer Vallow. Elmer called Great Falls, Montana home. Hethel was his first time out of the states.

"I just saw my first 'crapper,' fellas," Elmer told us. Dusty hadn't relinquished his bunk, so Elmer only joined us for meals and briefings.

"Hey, cowboy, I can believe that Montana still doesn't have indoor plumbing, but all our training stations did. You remember that, right after you got you first pair of new shoes," Jerry Shenkman kidded him.

"No, no Shenk. I mean a real Crapper."

Shenkman and I exchanged glances, then turned back to Elmer.

"Look, I'll show you," he said as he got up from the mess tent bench. "Follow me," and we did.

Our short walk outside took us to the Officers' Latrine. Vallow stopped at the first of the porcelain commodes that sat in a partitioned line, opposite the matching row of sinks.

"Now look here," and he pointed down to the top of the bowl behind the brass hinges that held the wood seat in place. And there it was, fired into the porcelain, "Thomas Crapper, London, England." Smiling broadly, Elmer fixed us two unbelievers in his stare. "I told you guys, and I'm willing to bet that these are the first crappers for you too."

We flew three missions together before Elmer went back into the Ready Replacement Pool, awaiting another spot.

* * * *

The family circle of our crew overlapped with other new circles of friends. Elmer Vallow was also a baseball player and joined our team, now expanded to ten guys. Our combined sources had gotten us more bats, balls, catcher's equipment, and even a set of bases created by an enterprising ground crew. Maj. Quinn secured space in an unused corner of the base for what passed as a ball field.

Col. Jimmy Stewart, who by age was somewhere between being a big brother and father figure, assumed the role of coach and manager. Dusty Rhodes was back in his beloved outfield, and I was at shortstop, with Elmer just to my right, playing third base. And I stayed in touch with my personal hero. Frankie Crosetti.

> *August 1, 1944*
> *Dear Frankie,*
> *I'm still here! The censors still won't let me say more than that. I hope your brother Johnny is doing fine. We've got 10 guys now and a coach /manager, Jimmy Stewart, the actor. He's a swell guy and got us our first bat from some Hollywood prop room. Anyway, the base has set aside a square of dirt for a field, and we practice as best we can. It looks like the Yanks are going to need two good months to make the series this year. About your team, Etten and Stirnweiss are knocking the cover off the ball and your four starting pitchers are still doing real good. We've got two fellas that I think could make the Bigs: my friends Jim Rhodes and Elmer Vallow. Your job at short-stop is safe for now. But when I get back, no promises. Say hi to the DiMaggio brothers for me.*
> *Bill Black*

14. Vengeance Weapons, June 1944

As the winds of war turned, the Germans began increasing use of their "V" for "Vengeance" weapons. The V-1 flying bombs began hitting England after D-Day in 1944. London and surrounding towns took a terrible pounding as this Second Blitz rained down. Antwerp and Liege, Belgium, also suffered under the same barrage. RAF Spitfires and our Mustangs could only shoot down some of these flying bombs.

In September the V-2 rockets came on scene. Lacking the accuracy to be used tactically, they were 'area weapons' for striking cities. Hitler and his high command knew that the war was lost but the damage and death the V-2s rained down on England might just get him a negotiated peace instead of an unconditional surrender. We were helpless to shoot them out of the sky because of their speed and trajectory. Stopping them on the ground was our only option.

On August fifth, our crew flew a mission against the V-1s. We headed for their launch sites in the Pas de Calais area near the North coast of France. Over 200 of our pals from nearby bases joined our four squadrons. German ground fire was heavy and brought down over 40 crews. Who died in the air, the crash or to Nazi bullets we seldom knew. Who made it back to our lines in France was another mystery. I could only hope that my comrades, known or unknown, made it out.

We never named our plane with any nose art. Probably because depending on how many holes or how much damage our planes received, we flew whatever planes were available. I felt that perhaps our luck was running out.

On our third mission over the French V-1 sites, my heated flight suit failed and so did Frisbee's. It was a long, cold ride back to England, but we made it.

One mission in mid-August turned us into a flying bomb when a fuel line was severed by ground fire. The liquid fuel and fumes that filled the plane were only one spark away from ignition. We stayed on bottled oxygen all the way home and vented the vapors as best we could through our waist gun windows. But we made it back.

* * * *

In the summer and fall of 1944, the V-2 Vengeance weapons began falling on London and near Norwich but never hit either the town or any of our bases. In northeastern Germany, on the tip of Usedom Island, where the Peene River empties into the Baltic Sea, was the Peenemünde Military Research Station. This was the main nerve of the German V-2 rocket program. Parts fabricated in underground factories elsewhere got assembled and launched from Peenemünde.

The Brits had been bombing Peenemünde since the fall of 1943. They hit an airfield and all three German research and testing facilities on the island. In late July of 1944, we joined the bombing. When the V-2s came into play, the 8th Air Force had made Peenemünde a priority target. The 200 bombing raids of July became 400 raids in August. We put the V-2 launch facility out of commission for weeks at a time. But with limitless slave labor, the launch sites got rebuilt and the rocket attacks resumed.

Our flight time to Peenemünde on August 24th was almost six hours. We were to be the second wave of bombers that day. Our B-24s would come in just after 375 B-17 heavies loosed their deadly cargo. If our timing was right, we'd catch the Germans away from their guns, busy dealing with fires and casualties.

Our 100-plane formation entered Germany on a course for Hanover. This false objective might further confuse the German defenders. Just north of the Hanover defenses, we banked left and headed straight for Peenemünde on the shores of the Baltic at Mecklenburger Bay. For the final 40 minutes of the flight, we were under continual anti-aircraft fire.

Frank got us through the leading edge of the anti-aircraft box. Lots of new openings in our aluminum skin, a bullet hole here, a shrapnel cut there, but we made it! We unloaded our 8,000 pounds of bombs.

As we banked left and headed for home, the outside of the German anti-aircraft box waited ahead. The black blooms of exploding shells filled the sky. I had us on our quickest route off the island below. Hopefully our passage through this garden of death would be brief.

A tremendous slap struck the plane. If there could be rocks in the clouds, we'd just hit one. I felt the smack on my left as the plane bucked. The intercom came alive in rapid overlapping shouts, questions, and profane cries. We were still aloft but seesawing through the air as our pilot and co-pilot struggled to level our flight. The shouts came too quick to identify the speakers.

"We're hit. Our one and two engines are on fire! Feather both props, now-now," came shouted words from the flight deck. The acrid smell of smoke hit my nose. Behind me, Ted Rossi had been knocked off his feet. His protective helmet and flak jacket probably prevented broken bones or a cracked skull. But the impact to his head kept him down. I was climbing out of my seat when my intercom speaker spoke to me.

"Red, what course…? Get us the hell out of here."

"Hold steady Frank, we'll be over water soon." Again checking over my shoulder, I added, "Rossi's down; Stan's checking on him."

Wind rushed up from Dusty's station in the nose of the plane, as other crew members checked in. "Cap, our nose turret took a hit from debris and a piece caught my leg." The unmistakable accent was Shenk. Then Dusty's voice came up from below. "Mi winder is busted, and da Nurden shot ta shit." Next Stan Grossi, the starboard waist gunner, came on. "Rossi is knocked out; I don't see any blood."

We could fly on two engines if we took no more damage. I climbed the two steps up to the flight deck. The flak blooms had stopped as we passed from the bay to the Baltic. "What's our flight time to Sweden?" asked Frank McGuffey with a quick turn of his head. Not wanting to raise any more alarm than we already had, he pointed down and tapped the fuel gage with his index finger. We were losing gas. Our two left engines were out, and their fires extinguished. But damages to fuel lines and tanks in the wing were starting to loom large.

"60." I shouted into his ear, over the noise and rush of wind. He nodded his understanding. Through the plexiglass I saw that two P-51s had chosen to stay with us. *God bless the sheepdogs.*

"Red, I don't want to put us in the drink. If we have to bail out or crash, I want it to be over land. How long to Denmark?"

"20 to the Danish coast. It's occupied territory. Skirt the coast and head northeast toward Sweden." Frank checked with Hawk Hawkins, who gave a thumbs-up to my suggestion.

"Okay." Keying the intercom, Frank McGuffey alerted the crew to the plan. "Guys, we'll be over land in about 15 minutes. We're losing gas, but I'm trying to get us to Sweden. I'll be skirting the Danish coast, so if necessary, we'll set down in Denmark and not the Baltic. Get your gear together." With the message delivered, Frank told Hawkins he was going to check on Shenk and Rossi. He instructed Frisbee to get the word out to our squadron about our situation and plan.

Rossi was still out cold, literally. We'd dropped down to maybe 1,000 feet as we skimmed the waves.

With our two left engines out, their generators no longer powered the heated flight suits. I'm sure everybody shivered in the cold as I did, but I heard not a word of complaint.

Jerry Shenkman had metal protruding from his right thigh. He'd fought the urge to remove the splinter, knowing that he'd be unable to stop the blood loss if he did. "Shenk, we'll get you some help on the ground if we need to," said McGuffey.

"I need some volunteers to help Shenk and Rossi." Three gunners spoke up, almost as one. Two gunners would help Shenkman and thankfully Rossi had revived. As the Danish coast came into view, Frank returned to the flight deck. Forty minutes to Sweden.

I was at my station. Dusty and I helped Shenk out of the nose turret and sat him carefully down by the front escape hatch. In 30 minutes, we'd skirt east of Copenhagen and cross the Oresund channel if our gas held out. It didn't.

"Listen up. We're on fumes. I'm taking us inland for an emergency landing. Everybody get out of your parachutes and have your escape packs at the ready. Buckle in or find something to hang onto. The landing may be rough. On the ground, you are on your own. Try to make it to the coast. Good luck to all of you," and the intercom went silent.

Frisbee's voice came over the intercom. "Captain, the 51s are leaving. They don't want to attract any more Germans on the ground."

McGuffey responded, "Thank them."

As even fumes ran out, I felt us clipping the tops of trees. Frank had put our landing gear down, perhaps a vain hope for a proper landing site. We shuddered with each hit, but no words came from anyone. When our landing gear hit a tree, the impact shoved us to the right and rocked the plane even more violently. And then the shuddering stopped as we glided the last 100 feet down past the forest and skidded to a stop in a stubble field. With only one landing gear strut intact, our plane sat tipped, one wing tip in the mud.

The escape doors opened front and rear. Croc eased Jerry Shenkman down into the waiting arms of Mac McCabe. It was every man for himself, but Crocker and McCabe walked their wounded friend off together. Outside, on the ground, I waited for Dusty, Frisbee, Rossi, Frank and Hawk. Quick goodbyes and good lucks ended. I headed back toward the cover of the woods. My friends scattered across the empty field, heading towards the Danish coast.

15. Somewhere in Denmark, August 1944

The forest lay 200 yards back from the field where we came to rest. Straight ahead, a road ran along one side of the empty field. I'd keep my wired flight suit on. I might need it for warmth if the weather turned cold.

In the controlled panic of our crash landing, I'd forgotten to unhook the Bail-out Kit from my parachute harness. I paused just a moment to consider: go back for it, or get away from the plane? The Germans would soon come looking for our crash site. I ran for the woods, leaving behind rations, a medical kit and other survival gear, like a compass.

I did get away with my Escape Kit and pistol with one clip of shells. There would be maps, the phrase card, ID card pictures and money. I hoped like hell that the kit contained Danish phrases and money. If I made it to the woods, I'd find out.

Inside the tree line, it was safe to stop and catch my breath. Half the trees were conifers, which I recognized from camping with my folks in the Sierras back home. Mixed in were ash, beech and elms that I recognized from some of the neighborhoods and parks in Stockton. I watched and waited, hidden behind the trunk of a pine. Had the Germans found our crash site? I silently prayed that they didn't have a search dog. I didn't want to put my first bullet into a dog.

Somewhere in the near distance, a single shot rang out. No one pounced on the plane. Had a passing patrol run into some of my friends? I prayed not. Time to find better cover, check my gear and see what help the stand of trees offered. The forest was a total unknown, so my eyes constantly surveyed my surroundings. I walked slowly, stepping quietly, trying not to break twigs or branches. I couldn't leave a visible trail if the Germans found my tracks away from the crash.

Mid-afternoon now. The August warmth brought out the smells of the pines and the mulch of the forest floor. I stayed away from the broken trees that marked the path of our descent. I kept a look-out for berries, mushrooms or edible ferns and especially water. Our pre-flight meal was nine hours ago, so I'd be hungry soon. Hunger was no fun but not fatal. Not so with thirst.

I circled the forest from inside its tree line. More a woodlot than a real forest, perhaps five acres at most. I'd spend most of the daylight there and finally hunker down for the night. I found a dry, sandy berm surrounded by thick ferns. I crawled through the base of the ferns so as not to leave a visible trail to my nest for the night. As night fell, I kept listening for trucks or shouting in the distance. Sleep did not come easily, and the full moon above did nothing to calm my nerves.

Sucking dew off fern fronds didn't work for shit, but at least it wet my mouth. I was glad that I kept on the insulated flight suit as the early morning got cold and damp. This was not camping, and not fun. Today I'd continue my circling of the woods. I'd stay near enough to the tree line and hope to get a mental map of the country, find a road sign and maybe a farm. The sunrise told me the direction of east and that would take me to somewhere on the coast. No food, no water, but no Germans yet, so I counted myself lucky. The sun shone down, so I stayed well in the shadows.

As I neared finishing my first circle of the woods, German troops came into view on the road beyond the field. I counted four of them. Two with binoculars began searching the horizon. I crouched behind a tree so as not to be seen. Two others stood at the crash site and had apparently checked the wreck for bodies. One had slung his rifle and held somebody's bail-out vest, probably mine. He rummaged through its pockets, stuffing cigarettes, chocolate bars and other plunder into the pouch pockets on his greatcoat. Spoils of war.

I guessed the four to be older, home guard types, finally pressed into service as the real fighters left. The Germans were busy trying to keep the Russians and us out of Germany. Thankfully my trail to the forest went undiscovered. Should I risk returning to the plane in hopes of finding water, rations or bullets? The bulging pockets of the soldier's coats meant little if anything remained inside.

I circled around the wood lot and returned to the nearest point between trees and road. I heard the four-man patrol drive off. The road lay 25 yards ahead, across an open field of tall grass. I'd be hidden if I low-crawled from the trees, so I did. The road was level with the field, so my path through the grass was not a beacon to my location. I lay still for 30 minutes, listening for trucks or worse, another gunshot. Parting the grass with my hands, I finally edged out to the pavement, searching for any signposts. There were none.

In the woods behind me was a passible hiding place, but nothing else. To my right on the other side of the curtain of grass was another stand of trees. Little more than a grove, but it was east, toward the coast. With no reason to turn around and stay hidden, that was my next target. Hungry but not injured or weak, my best chance was the grove.

* * * *

I carried my Escape Kit with me, tucked in a zipped leg pocket on my flight suit, just in case I had to make a running escape. The tall grass was dry and smelled like the San Joaquin Valley and home. A quick run was actually safer than a slow slither and I traversed the distance as fast as my best run from home to first base.

Time to survey my new position before moving on. What might I see on the other side of the grove or along the road? I saw the road when I circled around to the east side of the grove. Still no signage of any type. But there on the edge of the pavement lay a body. Even from this distance, I could see that the body wore an AAC heated flight suit. The gunshot last night and now this. But who? Which of our crew didn't make it?

Squatting inside the tree line amid the shadows, I looked and looked again. All day I watched the road, waiting for the man-hunters to reveal themselves, but no one emerged. Finally, as the sun dimmed into twilight, I walked out to the body. My worst fears were not only confirmed; they were amplified.

The body was Jerry Shenkman, our big Jew. A dark rosette of blood over his heart had soaked through the layers of his uniform and flight suit. His wounded thigh was still covered in a makeshift bandage, soaked through with dried blood. The presence of his body told me that Crocker and McQuade were probably prisoners.

The body told a vicious and hateful story. His faith had cost him his life. The Germans who killed Jerry had left the body as a message to the Danes and any downed Allied airman unlucky enough to cross their path. Wedged between his front teeth was one of his dog tags. The small metal rectangles we each wore showed our names, blood types and religious affiliation. Shenkman may have sounded suspiciously Jewish, but the six letters of "HEBREW" had cost him his life. Dried blood painted the word "Juden" on his forehead. At that moment, if my first bullet killed a dog, my next seven would go into as many Germans as I could kill.

* * * *

Hunger, thirst and an overwhelming anger about Shenkman's death now combined to force my hand. I had to move and find food and water. I could not stay still any longer.

From 20,000 feet up, the bombs we dropped were not personal. On the other side of the coin, being shot at by German anti-aircraft and Messerschmitt's was not them personally attacking me. Bad as it was, deadly serious as it was, it was not personal. But Jerry Shenkman's death — no, make that murder — seemed inexplicably personal and vicious.

What did I know, besides my hunger, thirst and which way was east toward the Danish coast? Nothing, really. So, I headed out, keeping to any cover available. Groves of trees, haystacks and ditches were my checkerboard of jumps as I moved east.

The first water I found was from a trough. It looked clean enough to drink, and I didn't care.

Ahead, across an open field, a farmhouse and barn appeared. The road where Jerry Shenkman died was at my back. The field offered no cover higher than six inches of grain stubble. But lack of options, combined with hunger, stirred me on. I listened for danger sounds, cars, planes or voices. Only the rustling of branches and bird sounds reached my ears. So, keeping low, I ran.

I jogged to the corner of the barn away from the road. Crouching there, I checked inside. It smelled of hay, dust, and animals. Still no food, but no alarming sights or sounds. Would I see a simple Danish farmer who hated the Nazis for invading his country back in the spring of 1940? Or was I unlucky enough to find Swastika flags or anything pro-German? When no alarm bells rang in my mind, I watched the house from the shadows inside the barn.

A form moved past a window. Someone was there, perhaps a savior. Possibly somebody that would use me as coinage to buy favors from the Germans. Hoping for the former more than fearing the latter, I kept my .45 in its holster. It was time to find out. I ran across the 20 yards from barn to house and knocked on the door. Guests and friends knock; enemies, especially Germans, kick the door open.

When the door did open, I was face to face with a middle-aged man. Brown hair crowned the rim of his bald head. A neat mustache and beard substituted for what hair had departed. I stood silent on his doorstep for a moment and then spoke a single word, "American." His eyes flared wide, and he stepped forward to look outside to the left and right. Then he reached out, put a hand on my shoulder and pulled me inside.

There at his kitchen table sat a half-eaten plate of food, a glass, and an unopened bottle of beer. He'd spoken not a word but motioned for me to sit in the empty chair across from his unfinished lunch. With unblinking eyes, he slid the beer over to my place. Then he turned his back to me and from the sink counter picked up a glass, a fork and a skillet. Was he going to hit me with the skillet? But he didn't.

Instead, the farmer sat back down. He slid his own plate across and passed the clean glass and fork over. Still silent, he gestured, his hand out, palm up, that I should eat and drink. I opened the beer bottle and poured half into each of our glasses. He smiled and again pointed to the plate of food.

"Spise," which, based on his gesture, I took to mean "eat." And I did.

I kept one eye on the skillet lying there unexplainably on the tabletop, within his easy reach. His half-glass of beer sat untouched. When he slowly reached for the skillet, I put my fork down and sat upright. He took the skillet in hand and held it up, showing me the bottom. Under its patina of scorch marks, across its center was the manufacturer's stamp, "ALCOA."

"Hvad er dette?" and he tapped the bottom of the pan. I exhaled sharply, not realizing that I'd been holding my breath. Again, he tapped the center stamp. Our eyes locked as I spoke.

"Aluminum Company of America," I said. He smiled at my answer and picked up his beer glass, signaling that we had something to toast. And as we did, he spoke again, "Godt." His smile, nod and inflection told me I'd passed some sort of test. I had knocked on the right door.

Now he brought to the table a plate of food for himself, bread and butter for us both. Pointing to himself he said, "Magnus" and I replied "William." Then I asked Magnus, "English?"

"En lille smule."

That sounded enough like "a little bit" that our communication moved haltingly forward in English. I removed the foreign phrase card out of my escape gear, and we communicated the essentials. I needed to get to neutral Sweden. Magnus told me to wait. He would try to help me but could say no more, except I needed to trust him now.

Rising from the table, he washed one fork, glass, and plate. One set of dishes waiting to be washed matched his solitary life. Two sets of dishes might be suspicious. As I looked on from my seat on his wooden chair, it occurred to me I was not the first downed flyer he'd helped.

Then Magnus took me back outside and over to the barn. Inside, he pointed to the hayloft that filled the back of the barn. "Under," and he pointed to the mound of hay that filled the loft. I nodded my understanding.

His hand grabbed my shoulder as I stepped up to the wooden ladder leading to the loft. Half speaking, half pantomiming, he communicated he had to go to make arrangements. I should hide under the hay if the Germans came. As we parted, I told him, "If the Germans find me, I hid here without your knowledge." I hope I got across that the only way I could repay his faith was by protecting him. Magnus left me alone, driving off in a vehicle that had been somewhere out of my sight.

* * * *

I stayed hidden inside the shadows of the barn. The August day was long and warm. The air inside the barn was still. The heat brought out the smell of the hay as a background perfume. I watched the dust and chaff float in a beam of sun that pierced the hay-loft window to the barn floor. If I closed my eyes, the aroma of the hay and the sounds of resident pigeons and swallows briefly transport me back to the San Joaquin Valley.

My watch had survived the crash. It was almost 8 PM when I heard a vehicle approaching. Cautiously, I peeked outside. Did I need to hide as far under the hay as possible and hope to escape discovery? It was Magnus, driving a small flatbed truck of uncertain age and origin. This time, the truck parked between the house and barn. Seeing me, he motioned to meet him in the house. Once inside, he pulled out one chair at his kitchen table and gestured for me to sit. I did.

He took a bottle of clear liquid from an upper cabinet. He set it down on the table and retrieved the glasses from the sink area. Two fingers worth of the liquid went into each glass. He sat down opposite me and raised his glass in a toast. White heat touched my lips and burned my throat when I tried to swallow. He smiled at my visible discomfort and said, "Aquavit, skol!" He downed the rest of his glass and offered a refill to me. I smiled but put up my palm in a universal signal of "No." Not the "*hell no*" I was thinking. All I'd felt was fire, and all I tasted was caraway.

As our communication skills improved, he signaled a pause. "Morning, I take you."

Fighting the Aquavit burn, I smiled and offered my glass in a toast. "Boat, tomorrow," and I nodded my understanding.

"Now, eat." As he got up to fix our meal, I got up, too. A polite guest offers to help, not to mention what a God-damned grateful guest should do.

* * * *

I retrieved the skillet from the counter next to the sink and returned to the table. I held the pan up with the bottom facing Magnus and tapped the "ALCOA" stamping. The skillet identification had been a test. Pantomiming a questioning look with my hands up-palms down and my mouth and eyes shaped into, I hoped, a universally understood questioning look. "Why?" I asked.

"Ah." said Magnus. He got up from the table and returned with a bible. He raised up one finger, showing a need for me to be patient while he searched the text. Finally, finding what he wanted, Magnus motioned for me to come around the table and see what he'd located. I realized what he was doing. Could the bible transcend the barrier of language through a shared story?

What I saw, all in Danish, meant nothing to me, so I turned my head and mimed confusion. Magnus pointed to the top of the page, underlining the biblical book reference with his fingernail. "Dommere" was the word. Magnus tapped the word and spoke it in Danish.

"Juh-jhihz" is what I heard. I repeated, "Judges?"

"Ja-Ja" and his finger moved from the book name *"Judges"* down the page, and tapped a boldly printed number, "12." Again, he slid his finger down the page, six paragraphs. Tapping first one, then another word, he turned his face to me and spoke. "Shibboleth-Shibboleth, guhd-guhd." Then his finger moved down two more sentences, and he tapped "Sibboleth-Sibboleth, no guhd-no gudh." It was a long time since church or sharing a family bible at home.

Again, I signaled confusion.

"Ah, Shibboleth-Aluminum." He emphasized how I'd translated 'Alcoa.' "Sibboleth-Alumin-ium," and then how the metal sometimes got pronounced as "al-u-MIN-eum" by the British and Germans.

I vaguely recalled the story of the men of 'Gilead' guarding a Jordan River crossing and questioning travelers to pronounce Shibboleth. The trifling difference in pronunciation revealed their enemies. Now I understood. "Yes-yes," I said, smiling my understanding.

He returned my smile. "Ja, Gohd." And our day ended.

My understanding of the skillet test increased later. I learned the Germans sent English-speaking soldiers, wearing captured American or British uniforms, out to Danish farms, as a ruse to discover and kill members of the Danish underground.

* * * *

When I woke at first light, Magnus stood on the barn floor, looking up at me sleeping in the hayloft. In his hands, he carried a complete change of clothes. Drab and visibly worn describes the shoes, socks, overalls, shirt and cap he brought, even underwear. These were my disguise. I changed and walked back to the house.

I didn't know what would come next, but I trusted Magnus. I expected to be hidden in a car or truck and smuggled to the coast. But how or what happened next was absolutely a mystery. He passed coffee and a plate of fried potatoes and eggs.

We communicated as we ate until he was satisfied I understood the plan and could do what I had to do. I repeated three words over and over until I sounded sufficiently Danish. "Ja, Far; Ja, Far." The words I should speak were "Yes, Father" and "hej," or "hi." No matter what I was asked, I was to respond only with some of those three words. I was only to smile and nod, the contented smile of a simpleton.

German patrols and checkpoints in occupied Denmark were thoroughly and aggressively searching all cars, trucks and wagons. I was going to hide in plain sight. Finally, I understood. I was the retarded son of the driver. I would ride next to Magnus in the truck's cab. If we got stopped, I should smile at the Germans and keep looking around. Whenever asked anything, give the same answers, "Ja, Far" or "hei." He took my watch and passed over items for my pockets: a single key and Danish candy. My watch stayed behind as unexplainable in the hands of a village idiot.

As we got up to go, I dealt with my last issue, the pistol. Take it or leave it? The decision was mine, but the risks shared. Hidden under my jacket or in the truck put us both at more risk. I resolved to have the pistol stay with Magnus. I slid the holstered pistol across the table. "For you," I said. He looked at the pistol and passed it back. Did he think I'd need it more than he would? I shook my head and again passed the pistol to him. Magnus now accepted the gun.

Copenhagen lay only ten miles northeast of the farm. At the town of Friheden, we met the first German checkpoint. Armed sentries approached the truck's cab while two others scanned the truck bed and undercarriage. Danish and German were ubiquitous in the area. When asked for papers by the sentry, Magnus produced his required identity card and explained that his son, "Albert," because he was disabled, had no papers.

The armed sentry on my side of the cab tapped on the door with his rifle barrel. "Papers," I guessed to be his question to me. My smiling reply, "Hei," brought forth a snicker. Then he banged on the door again and issued a command unintelligible to me, so I turned to Magnus. He smiled at his pretend son and gave a hand signal for me to get out of the truck. "Ja, Far," and I got out, still smiling and looking around. The two soldiers who'd searched the back joined the one who'd ordered me out.

"Hei," I smiled at the three who were snickering and laughing. One soldier stepped forward and forced me to my knees. My alarm transcended language, but I only voiced, "Far-far-far," and looked about in feigned panic. One sentry slapped the back of my head and laughed at my wide-eyed look of fear. Magnus came out of the cab and trotted to my side, the loving father protecting his disabled son. He patted my shoulder and spoke what probably were words of reassurance. Finally, the sergeant in charge ordered his men back to the trucks. He waved a dismissing hand for Magnus to put his idiot son back in the truck and drive on.

Magnus helped me to my feet, patting my shoulders and offering calming words. With us both back in the truck, at the barrier, the sergeant motioned him to a stop. He handed over a written pass to the driver, accompanied by "Es tut mir Leid," and allowed us to drive on. Out of sight of the checkpoint, Magnus turned to me and translated the sergeant's words, "He said, 'Sorry.'"

* * * *

Copenhagen was three miles further on. The pass got us through the next checkpoint and into the city. The city had avoided destruction by surrendering. Unlike Warsaw, bombed into submission, Copenhagen was intact. We drove to the docks on the waterfront.

We stopped at a wooden dock that jutted maybe 50 yards out. Along both sides of the dock, lines of small fishing boats busily unloaded the morning's catch. Magnus motioned for me to follow him onto the dock. As we walked, he made an unhurried inspection through the bins of fish, sometimes pointing, conversing or arguing with the captains about prices. At the last boat on the right, he shook hands with a crewman.

First, he looked down at the dock and then out into the channel. Seeing no foot or marine patrol, Magnus pushed me into the crewman's hands. He quickly ushered me onto the boat and pointed to a bench in the small cabin. I sat down and waited in silence. Through the cabin window, I saw Magnus receive a box of fish and exchange words with the fisherman. Then he was gone, back down the dock, but never forgotten.

* * * *

When the crewman returned, I shook his hand and said my name. His reply was, "No names please," and he lit a cigarette. I declined the offer to join him. "We go soon. Follow me."

His English was good enough to understand. He opened a locker in the small cabin. I saw an assortment of gear: rubber boots, oilskins, rubber gloves and wool caps. "Find boots and jacket that fit. Put on one of the watch caps and then come up on deck." I did as I was told. I found tall rubber boots, a black oil-skin waterproof jacket and knit cap.

"Good, you fit the part. It is a three-hour trip to Malmo at our best speed. You are my crew. It's safer and more believable than trying to hide you in a tub this small."

I understood his thinking. "OK, whatever you want me to do."

"Two things more. Do you smoke?" he asked. When I shook my head, he informed me, "Well, you're about to start." Taking a pipe and tobacco pouch from an inside jacket pocket, he handed both to me. "Since you don't speak Danish or German, you can't talk. It will give you away." That made sense to me.

"If you have a pipe stuck in your mouth, no one will expect you to speak. You are busy enjoying a smoke. See?" I did. He proceeded to give me a quick tutorial on pipe smoking, emphasizing how to keep the pipe lit, even in the sea breezes that were our constant companions.

"If we get stopped and a German speaks to you, ignore him. Unless, of course, he's pointing his gun at you and gesturing for you to put up your hands. Look to me for clues as to what to do. I'll nod or point or perhaps just a sideways glance. The Germans will just think you hate them, which is true, and are only listening to your boss. Me. Understood?"

Again, I nodded, "Yes."

"Last thing, yes. The E-boats think I'm a smuggler. It's true enough, but gin to Sweden and Aquavit to Denmark, no people." He smiled and winked, then pointed back inside the cabin to a wooden box stashed in a corner of the floor. "If I know the E-boat commander, I'm going to point and tell you in Danish to bring the box out and pass it over to the Krauts," and he stopped briefly. "The usual bribe." At this, we both smiled.

A fair breeze blew, raising white caps as we went across. I knew that the German E-boats patrolled coastal waters. I could only hope my luck held. I was about to find out.

The last days of August were warm and the sea calm under an almost cloudless sky. The boat's small diesel engine chugged away, its throb barely audible above the sea noises of parting waves and gulls circling overhead. For just a few moments, I allowed myself to be a passenger and focus on the natural world for as long as I could. Warmed by the sun and rocked by the sea, I fell asleep.

The taps on my shoulder came simultaneously with the words, "Wake up. Germans."

I blinked the sleep from my eyes and focused on an E-boat, rapidly approaching.

"Just sit still, unless I tell you."

Maybe 100 feet away, the E-boat slowed its engines and came alongside. I judged her to be 120 feet long, constructed of gray metal. She was heavily armed, with torpedo tubes, lots of mounted machine guns and probably 40mm cannons front and rear. I counted 14 crew members, either pointing the deck guns at us or standing at the rail aiming sub-machineguns in our direction. At their whim, we were both dead.

The wake from their powerful engines rocked our 30-foot boat violently, and I braced my feet and leaned again toward the cabin. I wanted to look as seasoned as my faux deckhand role required, or I was either dead or a prisoner. My anonymous captain recognized his opposite number standing on the flying bridge of the torpedo boat. He stood with his back to me at the far rail, one arm aloft in recognition. Finally, when the noise of the German's wake and engines quieted, he called across to the other captain.

"Horst, guten morgen!" "*Good morning,*" it sounded like. The captains continued, mostly in German, most of which made no sense to me. But I understood, nonetheless.

"Willie, was haben sie heute?" What I heard meant nothing, but when Captain Willie answered back "Gin für Malmö" I understood "Gin" and "Malmo." Captain Willie was a smuggler. Then he turned to me, interrupting my pipe lighting, and gestured to the wood box in the corner of the cabin. I fetched the box and was glad to see that by the time I was back on deck, all their guns were now lowered.

"Horst, a little something for you," and motioned me to the rail beside him. Willie's fishing boat and the E-boat were now side by side. Both hulls rose and fell together in the channel swells. Willie opened the hinged wooded lid. Inside the box rested 12 ceramic cylinders of Dutch Gin. He held one bottle aloft. "Gin this trip." No answer came down from Captain Horst. "I'll have Aquavit on my return, if you'd rather?"

Still no answer and I could see the German captain was discussing something with the two other officers up on the flying bridge. Willie and I shared glances, mine nervous and his more experienced and bored.

"Willie, I share with my crew, you know. I need two more bottles, please." What I heard next scared the shit out of me, when Willie lapsed into English.

"Horst, as you Germans say, 'business is business and Schnapps is Schnapps.' This is business. If I break a case for the extra two bottles, I can't sell it in Malmo." Both captains stopped.

Captain Horst was again in conference. I expected their guns to aim at us again any second when Willie spoke.

"If you can spare me a couple cans of petrol, you get your extra two bottles. Black market gas is expensive," and Willie skipped a beat. "Can we trade?" and another pause." Come across and I'll brew coffee. We'll work this out." Again, the German huddled with his officers. Then he raised his voice. "Fick dich du dieb."

And Willie broke into laughter. Later, he translated for me. "Said the pirate to the thief!"

"Pass up the gin, Willie and get on your way, but next time 14, understand?"

At least both Captains and all the gun-toting crew were smiling as I passed the case of gin to the waiting arms of a crewman. Without a word of warning, the E-boat diesels sprang back to life and its stern passed us. Its huge wake pitched me off my feet. My pipe clattered across the deck, now wet with spray. Back to my feet on the rocking deck, I gave the universal middle finger sign to the departing Germans. They returned my gesture and sped away.

"What did he say to you?"

"What do you think? Fuck you, thief." The barter between two competing crooks was frightening to me but routine for Willie. "Hey, give my pipe back. Don't let it go over the side."

Ninety minutes later, Malmo, Sweden, came into sight on the distant horizon. Prior to docking I returned my costume cap, boots and jacket to the gear locker for his next passenger. Captain Willie docked, and we parted as quickly as we'd met.

Over a parting handshake he told me, "Go to the police station," and pointed off the dock to the right. "Check in there. Good luck, my friend."

And I left.

16. Sweden, August 30 1944

The streets of Malmo were a combination of cobblestone walks, now joined by paver bricks. Two-story to four-story buildings lined the blocks. Bright colors on walls, and mature vines or bushes springing from planters in the cobblestones abounded. Each street-level shop had a descriptive wooden sign hung above its door. xw

Flower baskets and pots on windowsills added to the colors. The sweet smell of roses hung in the air. I crossed a wide canal via a centuries-old arched stone bridge and into a large open square. There, on one corner of the square, I saw the sign "POLISEN" above the image of a crown over a blue shield embellished with three smaller gold crowns. If I had any doubts, the uniformed men entering and exiting confirmed I'd found a police station.

I'd gotten to Sweden, a neutral country since 1939, as they had taught our crews. I was neither the first nor last Allied airman who'd reached their shores. To sell the two roles I'd played, first as retarded son and then as a smuggler's crewman, almost all of my American items had stayed behind. Hidden on Magnus's farm were my pistol, wristwatch, escape kit gear and all military clothing, even down to my underwear. Inside the station I went.

Before me was a counter manned by a uniformed officer. I knelt down and pulled off one shoe. My AAC identity card tumbled to the floor from under an insole liner. He turned to face me when I stopped opposite the counter. I held out the identity card, since my phrase card was back with Magnus. He took the card, examined it, and signaled I should follow him. And I did.

I sat alone in a small room. A desk and two chairs were the only furnishings. When the officer closed the door, I listened for the sound of a lock bolt being thrown, but I heard none. Neither in a cell nor locked in a room, I waited. It wasn't too long before the door opened. An English-speaking police officer filled me in on what would happen next.

"Lieutenant Black, welcome to Sweden. I will inform our contact with your embassy that you are here. Do you require medical attention?" I replied I was fine. "Good," and at that he passed over an envelope containing Swedish Kroners. "These are from your embassy."

"Outside, one soldier from our local army post will meet you. He will be your escort for the next two days. Your escort will first take you to lodgings that we keep available. You are free to walk about the town. The Kroners should be enough for you to get some clothes, eat and have a beer. Understood?"

"Yes sir," I responded.

"Take a day to relax. In two days, we'll put you on a train for Örebro, in our lake county. You will find some of your comrades there. Perhaps some are your friends."

Tonight, I would sleep peacefully, safe in a clean bed, or so I hoped.

* * * *

"To sleep: Perchance to dream: ay, there's the rub."
William Shakespeare

Frank McGuffy's voice fills my mind. "We're hit." Shouting now, so much shouting in my headphones and all around me.

"Red, what course...? Get us the hell out of here!"

My God, we're bucking, shuddering and my eyes can't stay focused.

"Red, answer me!"

"Hold steady, Frank. We'll be over water soon." *Great God, is that right?*

Now I hear wind rushing up from Dusty's station in the nose of the plane.

"Cap, our nose turret took a hit from debris and a piece caught my leg." It's Shenk. *What do I do?*

Now Stan Grossi's voice. "Rossi is knocked out. I don't see any blood."

What do I do? The shouting, the bumping. I don't know what to do. The bulkheads are gone and I'm there in the sky, flak blooming all around me.

"What's our flight time to Sweden?" screams McGuffey.

It is 60, isn't it? I need a minute—stop shouting!

"Red. Now. I need it now!"

"60," I shout over the noise and rush of wind.

"How long to Denmark?" *God, let me think.*

"How long to Denmark?"

Please.

"How long,...? NOW."

"20 to the Danish coast.

"Okay." McGuffy keys the intercom. "Guys, we'll be over land in about 15 minutes. We'll set down in Denmark. Get your gear together."

Suddenly, the flak is gone and all I see are trees coming directly for me. Good God, I'm alone and I see us clipping the tops of trees. I shuddered with each hit. But now there are no words, only screams.

Who—who's screaming? The wind, Shenkman, me? We hit a tree, the impact shoves me to the right and I rock forward. But the plane is gone, and it's just me gliding the last 100 feet down past the forest and seeing only a stubble field rushing at me. *I'm going to hit!*

And then I wake. Sweating, sobbing, safe in Sweden, but my mind had gone back to Denmark.

* * * *

The next day, my train trip to Orebro took seven hours, and I joined 18 other 8th AAC guys. They housed us, two men to a room, in Örebro Castle, the summer residence of the King of Sweden. They served three meals a day in the castle. We were free without escorts to roam the town, which sat between two deep lakes. Every month, Kroners arrived courtesy of our embassy. Almost ten weeks later, on December 1, 1944, with our number now swollen to 20, we were sent by train to Stockholm.

The Swedes had allowed a specially equipped B-24 to collect us. They had modified the all-too-familiar bomb bay to carry two rows of canvas seats. Here's hoping those bomb bay doors stayed shut on our flight to Edinburgh, Scotland, then back to Norwich and the 389th at Hethel.

During our brief transit stop there, I reconnected with as many of my friends as possible. What about my crew? No one knew anything about anyone. The news of some other friends' fates was better than I expected as the Germans were pulling back. Perhaps hardening a home defense? Perhaps something else; we'd see.

I soon found out I was not the only one visited by unwanted dreams. At least I wasn't alone. Some guys' dreams were of things done or undone. Other of things that were or might have been. And there were those whose dreams waited just inside their closed eyelids.

Some men escaped their dreams through booze. But booze only made things worse for me. So I chose poker. Our dreams accounted for so many late-night poker games.

* * * *

One day later, this time in a cargo plane, we flew from Norwich to the Azores, then on to Washington D.C. There I received a ration card, my accrued pay, a 30-day leave and my next set of orders. They sent me to Clover Field in Santa Monica, California. There, adjoining the Douglas Aircraft factory, the Army's 40th Aviation Division had its "Reclassification and Redistribution Center." But first I had my 30-days leave.

It took me two days to catch hops north to Stockton field. My proud parents and both sisters were waiting outside the taxiway when our C-47 landed. A single returning flyer on leave was no big deal. No flags, no brass band, but I was glad to see my family accompanied by Major Moen, who'd enlisted me so many years before.

My days were overfilled with Mom's cooking and the baked goods that showed up bearing notes of good wishes and congratulations. My downing, escape and route home rated a full column on page three of the Stockton paper. With the wars in Europe and the Pacific still raging, a military censor came out to the house. Even without his stern tones, I knew enough not to give much, if any, detail about how the Danish underground had helped me out of the country. I had lived the experience and shared the danger with these men, both patriots but neither of them soldiers. God bless them both.

Some nights I was visited by flashback scenes, pictures that I couldn't look away from.

I needed to reach out to several folks while in Stockton. Johnny Crosetti, my old boss, came around the counter and hugged me when I walked into his drugstore. We shared a cup of coffee at the fountain counter. I told him what I could about my experiences. He told me what he knew about other friends who'd also gone to war.

I asked him to pass along my best wishes to his family and brother Frankie, my baseball mentor. Separately, I wrote Frankie. I told him I appreciated his help and the introduction to his family friends, the three DiMaggio brothers. I told him I was giving up a baseball career in favor of a future as an Army pilot.

My last message was, "Please tell all the DiMaggio brothers to have the scouts for the New York Giants to keep a lookout for Jim Rhodes." All three of them were with Giants farm teams, and Dusty had more talent than I'd ever have.

My other contact was with fast Eddie Arroyo's parents. I'd stayed in touch with Eddie. He remained with the anti-submarine patrol unit for the duration of the war.

Smack in the middle of my leave time, the battle of the Bulge kicked off on December 16th. Like families with loved ones in service, like the old men playing dominoes under the trees in Victory Park, I followed the battle. I might soon be in an aircrew, dropping bombs or supplies on one side or the other of those battle lines. The battle raged on for another two weeks after my last kisses from Mom, Doris and Melba. Just as Dad had done years before, he drove me to the Southern Pacific station and shook my hand, hopefully not for the last time.

* * * *

The sun and the beach at Santa Monica, California, could put the war far from your mind. But it didn't, at least not for me. I had too many dreams intruding: the first time an anti-aircraft burst rattled our plane; the hanging 2,000-pound bomb; the cracking of wood and ripping metal as our plane crashed down through a Danish forest. They all plagued my sleep. Jerry Shenkman's defiled body. The taunts and slaps from soldiers delighting in tormenting the harmless, disabled person filled me with rage. I wanted to stay in the service and in the fight.

First came the Redistribution Board.

"Lieutenant Black, stand at ease," said the major overseeing the five-man board. "Your record speaks volumes, all good and damn lucky. Sixteen missions over Europe, until unlucky seventeen. Smuggled out by the Danish underground and repatriated through Sweden."

"Thank you, sir," I replied.

"You have crammed a lot into the past three years."

I let the observation stand and made no reply.

"We are here today to decide where you go next. You have earned the courtesy of our asking what you would like. We are confident you will do it well, whatever you choose. Have you given any thought to your future?"

"Permission to speak freely, sir?"

The hands out, palms up, gesture and his accompanying nod signaled I could begin.

"Flying as a navigator on all those missions made me feel kind of helpless, sir. Not being able to shoot back is bullshit. I'd like to train to be a fighter pilot and then go back into the fight." I'd said my piece in a plain, unvarnished fashion. Standing there at parade rest, I waited.

The answer came quickly. "Lieutenant Black, we don't have the power to grant your request, but we're going to do what we can to see you get it.

"We are forwarding your file to the Reclassification Board here at Clover Field, with our positive endorsement of your request. Make your pitch to them. We believe that you deserve reclassification for pilot training. Good luck."

Three days later, I stood before the Air Corps Reclassification Board and made the same request. The affirmative recommendation from the Redistribution Board, along with my service record, lay before the board members. I got my wish.

* * * *

I waited in a 'Casual Company' with other unassigned officers waiting for boards or orders. When my orders arrived, I was headed for the Mira Loma Flying Academy at Lancaster, California, for pilot training. For the next two months, I trained in a Boeing-Stearman Pt-13D two-seat biplane. After soloing, I had another choice. What did I want to fly? On the first of May 1945, I was catching a series of flights on my way to Steward Airfield at Newburgh, New York, for fighter pilot training. Less than a week later, on May 8, 1945, Germany surrendered. But we still had an enemy in the Pacific. I received a promotion to First Lieutenant now that I was a pilot.

Ten weeks of training followed. Sixty-five hours of ground instruction paired with 75 hours of flight time. First, I flew in biplanes, then single-wing trainers. My class moved through six different progressively faster planes, learning our craft.

Then came 30 days of gunnery training at Luke Field in Arizona. Now we flew 'almost real' fighter planes, AT-6 Texans.

One war was enough for now. I wasn't looking forward to going back into battle in the Pacific, but I would go if ordered. It was the fear of the Japs that had moved me to enlist. With MacArthur's troops well on their way to recapturing the Philippines, the horror of Japanese treatment of POWs was coming out. Letters from home had changed their tone from fear of a Jap invasion to outright hate for all things Japanese.

* * * *

On August 15, 1945, we all raised a glass in the O Club, celebrating V-J Day in the Pacific.

In my next letter to Eddie, I asked his plans. He was coming back to Stockton once released from active duty. Exactly when, who could tell. He'd use the new G.I. Bill to enter college. He still loved baseball but had not set his sights on being a professional.

We affirmed our long-ago deal: July 4th at Stockton Joe's Italian Restaurant. We hoped for next year if he was back and I could get leave.

We never kept our date. His plane went down in the Atlantic on a routine training mission. He didn't make it.

17. Between Two Wars, October 1945

What plane would I be flying now that I was a fully trained fighter pilot? One of my beloved P-51s or one of the new jets that were rolling off our production lines and into service? Neither, actually. I was flying a desk as an Administrative Officer in a Training Squadron at Chanute Field in Rantoul, Illinois.

Our training squadron turned out jet engine mechanics, so I sat in on as many classes as I could manage. I stood next to students as they learned, literally, the nuts and bolts of jet engines. What I heard and saw might save my life somewhere down the line. And if I was willing to spend the time, chances to fly abounded. I volunteered to ferry planes from one field to another.

In June 1947, an opportunity came to get qualified on the twin-engined A-26 Invader, and I jumped at the chance. That is one helluva plane, I'll tell you. I had a 30-day Temporary Duty assignment approved to Randolph Field in San Antonio, Texas. I was about to add two planes to my list of qualifications: P-51s and A-26s.

For the first time, I would get behind the stick of a P-51. Where our B-24 had been a draft horse, here was a racehorse.

A-26 Invader Ground Attack Fighter/Bomber

* * * *

Randolph Field adjoined Lackland Field outside the city of San Antonio. In my Transient Officers Quarters was a "Things to See and Do in San Antonio" booklet. The Alamo became number one on my list for the weekend. I also keyed on an advertisement for the United Services Automobile Association. The ad began "Randolph Field's Own." I made a note to learn what I could about the USAA while I was in town. My shoes shined and my Class B khaki trousers and shirt freshly pressed, I drove my Buick convertible down from Chanute Field.

Randolph Field occupied what had been a large horse ranch. The odor was gone, but the peeled-pine fencing around the parking lot fit the image. I asked for directions from the first person I saw wearing a flight suit. The route to the O Club was simple and the cue, "It's the old hacienda. You can't miss it, all adobe and lots of tiles," gave me a visual. At the end of a tree-lined boulevard, there it sat. I parked and started in.

To the right of the carved double entry doors was a bronze plaque commemorating the Rancho Moreno hacienda, built in 1830 on the Moreno family's horse ranch.

I showed my ID card to the Duty Officer at a podium just inside in the cool adobe shade.

"Welcome, Lieutenant Black. Is this your first time with us here at Randolph?"

I replied it was.

"This is the home of USAA, and those good folks always buy new visitors their first drink." From a box kept under the podium he removed a regular, theater-style admission ticket. "Just give this to Mr. Nolan, our barman, and he'll serve you. Welcome."

I headed for the bar and took a stool.

Behind the polished, dark wood of the long bar top, a barman approached. French cuffs showed under the sleeves of his crisp white waistcoat. His lined face, of indeterminate age, was the color of saddle leather, but precisely combed gray hair still covered his head.

I passed across the red paper ticket.

"What can I get for you, sir?"

"Martell's and soda," I replied. Somewhere along the way, I'd acquired a taste for French Cognac. Since any day's drink might be my last, I only drank 'the good stuff.'

I watched the barman select the blue-labeled Martell's bottle. He removed a small bottle of Schweppes Club Soda from below the bar top and stopped. Two questions followed, of the type only asked in the finest watering holes where both barman and customer knew their stuff.

"Short or tall, sir?"

"Short," I replied, and a heavy-bottomed low-ball glass appeared.

"On the rocks sir?"

Again, I responded in the affirmative, and crystal-clear cubes of ice went into the glass, followed by a generous double shot of cognac. Then a splash of club soda and one quick stir with a long-handled swizzle stick, and the glass was placed on a coaster in front of me.

A dish of salted green nuts with pointed ends appeared next to the drink. "Salted Pepitas, sir, a local delicacy."

When I continue to stare at the seeds, the barman reassured me. "Roasted and salted Mexican pumpkin seeds."

"Thank you, Mr. Nolan," and I nodded in appreciation for a master of his craft. He nodded his recognition and stepped away to busy himself with other customers.

I frequented the club during my days at Randolph. Pete Nolan soon recognized me, knew my drink and that I was a good tipper. Late one evening I asked about USAA.

"It's a self-financed company providing auto insurance to military officers and their families. It started right here, back in 1922."

"Who started it?"

Pete leaned over the bar toward me, not wanting to broadcast his response. "A bunch of drunk fighter pilots who couldn't get insurance for their sports cars." Pete was my kind of bartender, a professional and a no-bullshit guy.

* * *

Next at Randolph Field, I got to fly the Cadillac of fighters. There it was, a P-51D Mustang. My up-close inspection didn't disappoint. From the six exhaust ports on each side of the nose, I knew that under the cowling sat a Packard-Merlin engine. I could fly straight and level at 470 miles per hour and exceed 500 in a dive.

I climbed up into her cockpit. The plexiglass molded canopy gave me an unobstructed field of vison. Only two narrow posts separated me from a seat in the clouds. Nothing blocked my lines of sight in any direction. The designer must have been a fighter pilot who understood the absolute need to see the enemy, preferably before he sees you.

The controls were well placed and readable. Yes, a fighter pilot had designed this plane. I flipped on the magneto switch and fired up the 12 cylinders of Rolls Royce-designed power plant. The tower cleared me to move, and I touched the throttle to taxi out.

The Mustang jumped ahead, her power and response unlike any plane I'd flown. Holy shit! I was on a racehorse, and a gentle nudge was all she needed to move. Who was training whom became unsure.

Gently now, I moved the throttle, and we were soon off the taxiway and onto the concrete runway. A final check with the tower and I throttled up to full power. It pinned me back against my seat, and we were airborne. Landing gear up and I banked right, heading for my designated flight path.

Carefully, I tested the Mustang's responses to my touch: instantaneous. Bank, dive, climb, anything I ask of her she gave, and then some. How do I describe this? Mind, body and plane worked as one. I didn't need to think before I move the controls. It all seemed to happen naturally. If I looked there, I was there. No whip or spurs needed with this mount.

* * * *

The A-26C Douglas Invader was my first twin-engine plane, and I liked her the moment I laid eyes on her. The "A" signified "Attack." Smaller, lighter and faster than the Liberator, it was to replace the A-20 Havoc as our ground attack plane in the next war.

She sported two 18-cylinder Pratt and Whitney supercharged Wasp rotary engines, the same engine that powered the B-24 Liberators, but on the smaller plane the two Wasps produced more speed: 50 miles per hour extra. She was designed to strafe ground targets, so there were four underwing gun packs of twin .50 caliber machine guns, and the nose gun pack was something to behold.

"Lieutenant," said my instructor, "the nose gun packs can be six- or eight-gun units. 50 caliber machine guns, or either 20- or 37-millimeter auto-cannons, and a shitload of ammo. Whatever the mission calls for, we can outfit this baby. Also, below the nose guns, there is a bomb sight, and her belly will hold 5,000 pounds of bombs.

From the moment I climbed into the cockpit, I loved the plane. My navigator sat beside me and worked the radio, too. Our third man was a bombardier who doubled as the ammo loader. This was a pilot's plane: fast and maneuverable. Not a racehorse, but more of a hunting hawk. Nothing on the ground stood a chance against this plane. The lethal combination of cannons and machineguns made it a devastating ground attack weapon. I'd gladly fly one of these babies any day, and being qualified on single and twin-engine planes made me more valuable to the AAC.

18. Change Is in the Wind, September 1947

The rumor mill was grinding at full speed; a big organizational change was about to arrive. Congress passed the National Security Act of 1947. The base commander at Chanute, and probably all base commanders, announced that the Army Air Corps was to become the United States Air Force in September. On September 18th, it became official.

So, what would change? Our organization structure: Flight, Squadron, Group, Wing and so on? Nope. A Fighter Squadron would still have the same number of planes. Brown shoes were replaced by black shoes. "Captain" became abbreviated to "Capt." Instead of "Cpt."

We changed a few names. The P-51 became the F-51. "P" for "Pursuit" became "F" for "Fighter." "A" for attack became "B" for Bomber. Chanute Field became Chanute Air Force Base. Our beginning rank was now "Airman" instead of "Private." If you said it fast, Airman sounded fine. But spoken slowly we had Air Man.

We had no end of fun with Air Man. Almost everybody came of age watching "The Rocketeer" serials. I thought our Air Man could help The Rocketeer and Commander Cody in their never-ending fights against evil. Besides, Rocketeer's girlfriend was a cartooned image of Betty Page, the queen of so many barracks wet dreams.

Oh yes, and they changed the color of our uniforms and headgear. I suspected a cabal of clothing manufacturers was secretly behind the change. Oh, and don't forget their corps of co-conspirators: sign painters, printers, shoe companies and the sleeve stripe producers.

* * * *

Throughout 1948, I continued to fly whenever I could. I picked up planes at the factory and delivered them to their assigned squadrons. My administrative position at Chanute Air Force

Base opened doors to flying as part of evaluating new models of aircraft.

Every pilot I knew closely followed world events that might, at any moment, plunge us into another shooting war. The Russians set off their A-bomb in August 1949. Mainland China fell to the Reds in the same year. It looked to planners above my pay grade that Korea might be a flashpoint. I was ordered to McClelland AFB in California to qualify on another aircraft, the F-82 Twin Mustang. I set about educating myself about the F-82.

F-82 Twin Mustang Fighter

From my desk at Chanute, I had access to information. I knew from the war years that we developed the P-51 as a long-range fighter escort. I also knew that our F-80 Shooting Star jet came online at war's end. Almost five years later, it would be replaced by the F-86 Sabre jet, then in final testing. Fine planes, except neither had a great range. With drop tanks for extra gas, the F-80's range was 1,000 miles round trip. For interceptor purposes, it had only a 600-mile range and couldn't stay over targets that long.

The F-82 Twin Mustang with drop tanks had a range of 3,500 miles. Even without drop tanks, it tripled the range of our frontline jet. It could deliver four, 1,000-pound bombs or carry twenty-five, 50mm. diameter rockets, besides its six internally mounted machine guns. This was our plane designed and built to accompany heavy bombers over the great distances of the Pacific to bomb Japan.

The newly minted Strategic Air Command used squadrons of Twin Mustangs as long-range escorts for their bombers. They were a stop-gap plane to be used only until a suitable jet replacement came online. The rare propeller planes not taken by SAC would go to war as night fighters if a Korean conflict kicked off, because this was what we had. These squadrons flew planes painted all black and equipped with a radar module mounted under the center wing section.

* * * *

Parked at the side of the runway, the glossy black paint job called to mind "menace." Captain Bill Bouma was my flight instructor, a qualified F-82 pilot himself. He'd be in the right-side radar man's cockpit of the Twin Mustang, with me on the left in the pilot's seat. For my honeymoon flight, we'd go up in daylight. I liked the idea of getting the feel of the plane before taking on the new task of flying at night.

We walked around the Twin Mustang bodies and stopped at the huge black cylinder suspended below the center wing: the radar pod.

"What do you call that thing, Captain?"

"We call that 'the dong'." That got a smile and a nod from me. "The radar can be set to show ground targets or switched to airborne bogies. Not a bad deal because it gives you options. Targets of opportunity, such as reports of a truck convoy."

I pointed up to the 6 exhausts on each side of both engine cowlings. "Allison V-12s?"

"I flew Mustangs in Europe. Loved 'em. The Allison is not a Merlin. You'll see," and Captain Bouma stopped there, perhaps not wanting to taint my judgment by emphasizing his own assessment. "Shall we take her up?"

I nodded in agreement and walked back to the left-side cockpit. Our ground crew removed the wheel chocks, and I taxied out. We checked our communication link, and I made one last contact with the tower for clearance. When I hit the gas, the left-side engine backfired and expelled a big puff of smoke.

Bouma's voice rasped in my earpiece. "They do that. Go."

I throttled up slowly like I had in the P-51, but the Twin Mustang barely budged. I pushed the throttle harder, and the plane began to move forward and gain speed. Soon we were aloft. The two Allisons did equal the Merlins' power and speed. Then it came to me. The difference was in the responsiveness. The Merlin wanted to go fast; not so the Allison. It needed more deliberate throttle pressure. I'd adjust.

When we were back on the ground and the day's lesson over, the captain asked, "What do you think?"

I took a moment before answering. "Not bad when I got up to speed, but a lead sled at low power."

He nodded in agreement. "Yup, not a Mustang, but a suitable plane anyway." Then, with a shake of his head, he added a final comment, "And it's what we've got. Any other observations?"

"Just two. It will take some getting used to having the other fuselage right there in my peripheral vision. I keep feeling we're about to collide."

Bouma grinned. "You'll get used to it. What else?"

"The gyro for reading my inflight attitude reads the opposite of all the other planes I've flown. When it looks like I'm rising, I'm descending. That will take some getting used to. But like you said, we fly what we got."

At the end of our training time, Capt. Bouma certified me as a qualified F-82 pilot.

19. Orders for the Orient, April 1950

Finally, the orders I was expecting came through. I was going to the 51st Fighter Wing at Kadena, Okinawa. I was to pick up my plane, one of the new F-82 G Twin Mustangs, back at McClellan AFB in Rancho Cordoba. I hadn't been there in years. They brought the planes up from the North American Aircraft plant at Inglewood, California. I would transit to Korea and deliver my plane at the same time. At McClellan, I'd also meet my radar operator.

I had a week's worth of work before being due at McClellan in two weeks' time. Clear my quarters, deal with finance issues and get lots of new shots. Diseases endemic in the Orient had not been likely risks in Europe or the States. I also wanted to learn what I could about my new unit.

After the war, we had assumed responsibility for Japan's defense. The 51st Fighter Wing had been in Japan since 1947. The 68th All-Weather Squadron was trading in their World War II Black Widow night fighter. The F-82G's were not what we wanted, but the Lockheed F-94C Starfire jet night fighter, prototyped in July 1949, was not due to come online until late 1951. You go to war with what you have.

I left Chanute on a Monday morning and headed west on Illinois-7. My 1949 Buick Super 8 convertible should make the trip in about 40 hours. I traveled with the top down whenever I could. The red paint job and saddle leather interior would need a good cleaning when I arrived, but I didn't care. Its big chrome grill always reminds me of a bulldog with a bad under-bite, but I loved the car. The seats felt like sitting on a good sofa.

I drove across Iowa and Nebraska and caught the corner of Wyoming before dropping into Utah. Crossing northern Nevada, I jogged down to Deeth to visit Uncle Charlie and Aunt Nini. Uncle Charlie still farmed the land where my grandfather had raised cattle. They had not rebuilt Deeth after the 1920 fire that ravaged the town and caused my family to move to

Stockton. All that remained of my dad's store was a cement foundation.

No matter where I laid my head, I was carrying the war in my dreams and couldn't seem to put it down. I worried about my dreams interfering with my clarity in the single combat between fighters.

Over the Sierra Nevadas and across Donner Pass, I was only hours away from Stockton and my folks. After the dust and sage of the high desert, the foothills and Central Valley were a sea of green. A million fruit trees perfumed the air, all seeming in bloom at once. I called home from Reno on my last night of travel. "Expect me for dinner tomorrow."

* * * *

Dad and Mom had sold the chicken farm on Cherokee Lane during the war. A factory job lured Dad into town and the folks bought a small house on Gertrude Street. I'd be seeing the house for the first time. Dad gave me directions to find their new place, which is easy to do in little Stockton.

Gertrude Street's asphalt was in bad repair. Like so many things, they'd diverted asphalt oil to the war effort. When I turned into their graveled driveway, Dad emerged through the gated white picket fence. I parked just ahead of the white, wooden single-car garage.

"Your mother is inside. We'd best go in." He turned and headed back into the yard, not apparently hearing me when I spoke.

"Let me put up the top on the Buick, so she doesn't fill up with dust." Right away, I noticed Dad's hearing, which had always been bad, had gotten worse. Probably a casualty of working in a machine shop. I raised the tan convertible top, rolled up the windows and left my two bags in the car.

Inside the fence, a cement path joined the two steps up to the back door. The lawn inside the cement walk was a pale green Bermuda grass. I went in the back door, passing through to the kitchen where Mom, in her same calico apron, stood at the sink. Drying her hands on a dish towel, she crossed her kitchen and hugged her baby boy.

One of us had gotten shorter. I could see threads of gray on the top of her head. Then she smiled. "Your sister Melba will be here for dinner. Let's join your father in the front room." My oldest sister Melba, still unmarried, shared an apartment with another gal, who also worked in the county health department lab.

Warm afternoon sun lit the room from windows on two sides. While their residence had changed, it looked like their furniture had not. Dad sat in his overstuffed armchair. On the low table to his right sat a gunmetal tobacco humidor, a small pipe rack, and a brown glass ashtray. The room was infused with years of smoke. The aroma of Mixture 79 brand Tobacco was everywhere.

I sat down on the couch, and Mom took her chair next to Dad's end table. I soon understood why. A tablet and pencil rested on a corner of the table. When she spoke, she faced him and spoke slowly. He was reading her lips. She wrote out any words he didn't understand. Dad's voice often verged on too loud for the inside, but unable to hear himself, he didn't know. The years had not been kind to my folks.

Mom excused herself. The welcome home dinner had to be finished. Dad loaded his pipe from the humidor. Being careful to get his attention, I spoke as slowly, enunciating each word without trying to exaggerate his disability. I pointed at the gray metal humidor.

"New. Did you make it?" I'd succeeded in being understood.

"Made that down at the plant," he answered. "Let me show you the place," he said. I nodded and rose from the couch. With his pipe in one hand and a couple of wooden matches in the other, he gave me the tour. A hallway paralleling the living room connected bedrooms at either end, with a tiled bathroom in between.

I followed him back through the kitchen, where Mom had set four places at the chrome, Formica-topped table. Once outside, Dad lit his pipe and explained between puffs, "Your Mother doesn't like me to smoke in the house." The smell of every cushion and inch of drapery in the living room argued that the old man just ignored her wishes.

I looked through a side door into the freestanding wooden garage. No car. The interior was all storage and drying racks for walnuts. Crude wooden shelves sagging under the weight of canning jars filled two walls.

The lot was large: a good half acre. On this side of a wire mesh fence, a covered patio shaded a wooden picnic table. Flower beds formed a neat border to the lawn on its two remaining sides. A wood and wire chicken coop shared the back wall of the garage. The chickens ate bugs from the garden. Mom and Dad ate their eggs and occasionally ate one of them. The rest of the far back yard was planted in the neat rows of a home victory garden. Chard, carrots, squash and beets covered the ground up to a tall row of berry vines.

The tour concluded in the front yard. The leaves and limbs of a large walnut tree filtered the heat of the day. The front porch of red painted cement was three steps above the front lawn. A sloping wood overhang shaded the front windows and a metal-framed glider swing. We were headed back inside when Melba arrived by taxi.

Over dinner, I got the family news. My sister Doris was now a married woman, Mrs. Philip Scott. She had moved into her husband's house in San Bruno. She worked as a secretary in San Francisco for Seaside Oil, the retail brand for Tidewater Oil. Today being Thursday, I understood why my sister and new brother-in-law could not be here for dinner.

I knew Frankie Crosetti was still the Yankees' shortstop. Melba was also a baseball fan. In a recent San Francisco Seals game against our hometown Stockton Ports, two of the DiMaggio brothers played in the outfield along with an unknown named Jim Rhodes. I told them all my Dusty Rhodes stories about 'southernese', playing ball with Jimmy Stewart and the hanging bomb. This was the first I knew Dusty had made it back and was now one step below the Bigs. That news was as good as Mom's apple cobbler.

I'd never made the effort to discover the fate of the rest of our crew. I didn't want to know if any more of my friends had been killed. The fact that Dusty had made it somehow seemed to balance the scales for Shenkman.

Melba agreed to go with me to Sacramento, drop me at the base, and care for my prized convertible until I got back to the States. I sent my Buick home with her that night so she could get used to it.

She was back at 8 AM the next morning. We made the one-hour drive through the fields, orchards and vineyards of the valley, and there we were at McClelland.

"Take care, Sis," were my parting words.

"You take care, Little Brother," and then she and my convertible vanished.

20. December 1949

McClelland AFB is located in Rancho Cordoba, a suburb of California's capital, Sacramento. While I got checked out on the Twin Mustang, I'd find time to see all my family.

The orders to McClelland stated I should check in with the 6303rd Air Bridge Group. I recognized them as the outfit that arranged the delivering of planes. With my pigskin valise in hand and a garment bag slung over my shoulder, I walked into the Security Office to the right of the two-lane entrance street.

The Air Police Sergeant behind the counter saw the silver bar on my collar. "Good morning, sir." The luggage told him I was transferring in or reporting for Temporary Duty to McClellan. "ID and orders please, sir."

I set my valise down and looked for a place to hang the garment bag. I settled for draping it across the arms of a chair.

My military ID assured him I wasn't a Russian spy. The order retrieved from the inside pocket of my uniform coat explained my presence at his counter. "Lieutenant, I'll have one of my guys take you over to the 6303rd. They are at the far end of the base. Not really a walk, sir."

I took him up on the offer and got a jeep ride to my report in. For the moment my priority was being on time or early.

The military was never much for aesthetics in their architecture. The 6303rd had the entire first floor in a two-story wood building that looked like a converted barracks. I repeated my check-in by showing my orders to the staff duty NCO.

"Welcome to McClelland, Lieutenant Black. You are right on time, sir. We have a room reserved for you in our transit barracks. I'll have a driver take you over and you can get checked in and drop your gear."

I thanked him.

"Do you need anything, sir? A meal, PX?"

"No, I spent last night at my folks' place in Stockton and had breakfast already. Point me to the latrine and then I'll make a quick stop and then be ready to go."

"Down the hall, second door on the right. You can leave your bags here and I'll have them loaded up and a jeep out front. The driver will wait and bring you back here after you're checked in."

I thanked him again. "Never miss a chance to pee, sergeant. That's a little flight crew secret."

* * * *

Forty minutes later, the duty driver returned me to the 6303rd. "Sir, we have a dozen officers coming in. When you finish with your briefings today, I'll be outside to take you back to your Q. I will be there at 0800 tomorrow to bring you gentlemen back here."

I thanked the driver for the heads up.

Unsure about what was on schedule for today, I had worn my Class B khaki uniform and garrison cap. I carried a small canvas bag with my flight suit and boots inside, just in case.

The NCO at the front desk immediately directed me to a second-floor conference room in the headquarters building. A rectangular table lined with chairs occupied the center of the room. In front of each chair was a closed manila folder. A large blackboard and maps of the Pacific filled two walls. Half a dozen other officers — captains and lieutenants — were engaged in conversation.

A few acknowledged my entrance with turned heads as I joined the group. "Good morning," said one officer as he extended a hand. "Ralph McIntosh."

I returned the greeting and joined the cluster of flyers. Everyone introduced themselves and we briefly lapsed into small talk as more men, in ones and twos, joined the group. The last man through the door sported the gold oak leaves of a major. He walked to a lectern and turned to face us.

"Take a seat, please." He waited until we were all in chairs around the table before continuing. "Good morning. I am Major Hall. Please open the folder in front of you." The major walked us through the contents of the folder: our flight plan for island hopping across the Pacific.

Why the F-82 was created became crystal clear when I studied the distances between our island stops. With auxiliary fuel tanks, it could fly almost 3,500 miles. They assigned us radio frequencies for in-flight communication between planes. A list of tower frequencies at each stop and Naval rescue frequencies completed the list.

The flight route planned one-day layovers at each of our four refueling stops. Pilot fatigue was more of a worry than running out of gas. The saving grace in our planes was having two qualified pilots. In the long stretches of open water, a nap might be necessary and having someone to speak to was desirable. I liked the two flights with staggered departure times. The other planes could direct rescuers to a downed aircraft if necessary.

Day one, San Francisco to Hickam AFB, Hawaii, would be 2,400 miles and six hours flight time. Day two, Hickam to Midway, was 1,100 miles and three hours in the air. Then Midway to Kwajalein in the Marshall Islands was 1,650 miles and 5 hours aloft. The last leg was the longest, Kwajalein to Okinawa, 2,800 miles and a seven-hour flight time. Thank goodness for the relief tubes we had. As long as the air was smooth, hitting the funnel was not a problem. Last but not least was a list of pilot and radar operator pairings.

"In case some of you didn't already meet the rest of the group, acknowledge when I read out your name," said the major. He read out the pairings. My future co-pilot and radar man, as yet unknown to me, raised a hand at the sound of his name, First Lieutenant Enrico Banducci. When my name got called as his partner, I did the same. Alphabetical order?

For the rest of the day, each pair was to inspect, identify by its serial number and test fly their planes. No surprises over the Pacific, please. When the meeting ended, Banducci and I paired up.

"Call me Rico," was his introduction.

I grinned. "Call me Red."

Individually, we were brought into the Flight Surgeon's office. First came a series of questions. What was the longest flight I'd ever made in a fighter plane? Was I a coffee drinker? Then the purpose of the consultation became clear.

"Lieutenant, you are about to embark on long flights in a confined space over water, with no visual stimulation, no variety." He waited, hoping that his message sank in. "The sky and the water can start to look the same, and that's disorienting. Or it might make you drowsy. You nod off, just for a moment. When you snap awake, you may be confused about up and down. Blue above, blue below. Do you take my point?"

"Yes, sir; don't fall asleep."

His response, a slow nod. "I can give you some 'go pills' for the flight. They will keep you awake if you feel yourself about to doze off." He placed a small pill bottle on the desktop between us. "Just in case," and with that, his demeanor changed back to all business. "Dismissed."

I put the bottle in a pocket of my flight suit.

* * * *

Rico had already been in to see the flight surgeon, so we left together and went to our plane. We did a safety inspection walk-around and checked with the crew chief. She was gassed and ready to go.

"Rico, now that we've kicked the tires, how about we take her for a test drive?"

"Good idea. Every plane I've ever flown had a personality: quirks, things that you only find out in the air. Better now than later, so let's go."

We put our new ride through its paces over the valley farms, above the coastal mountains and along the California coast, then back to McClellan.

"How does she handle, Red?"

"Smooth as Baby Jesus in velvet pants, once I got her up to pace. She's a bit of a slug at low speeds. How was it from your side?"

"It takes some getting used to, not having all the flight controls. I've got just enough to land, if you're passed out and we're lucky. Landing gear, flaps and throttle. That's all I've got."

"I'll try not to pass out on you. Fair enough?"

"Deal."

We set her down and headed for the O Club. One drink later, I excused myself. There would be lots of time in the air for better, longer introductions We agreed to meet for breakfast tomorrow, before our planes departed on our island-hoping transit.

* * * *

We met at the Officers' mess at 0700 the next day. We each brought along a thermos of coffee; I had another filled with water. Banducci probably had red wine in his second thermos, but I didn't ask. My valise and garment bag rode in a storage compartment situated forward of the rear landing-gear well.

It was wheels up at 0800 with our two other traveling companions in "Twins One."

Our flight leader, Capt. Walter Williams, partnered with Delbert Henley riding in the other seat. Banducci and I tucked in behind him on the left. Carroll Peterson piloted our third bird, and Gerry O'Donnell manned the radar. Soon after we got aloft and headed for the California coast, I heard a click over the radio.

"Listen up fellas," I recognized Walt Williams' voice. "You all had the meeting with the flight surgeon and were offered the white go-pills. It is your business if you take them or not."

Okay, no judgments here from the boss.

"A word from the wise. If you rely on the go pills and don't keep taking them, when they leave your blood stream, you will fall asleep before you know it. I lost a friend to that scenario. So,

I have another cup of coffee if I feel the need." Silence followed, and then Williams came back into our ears. "Only one of you in each plane can use the go pills."

Banducci and I both decided not to use the pills.

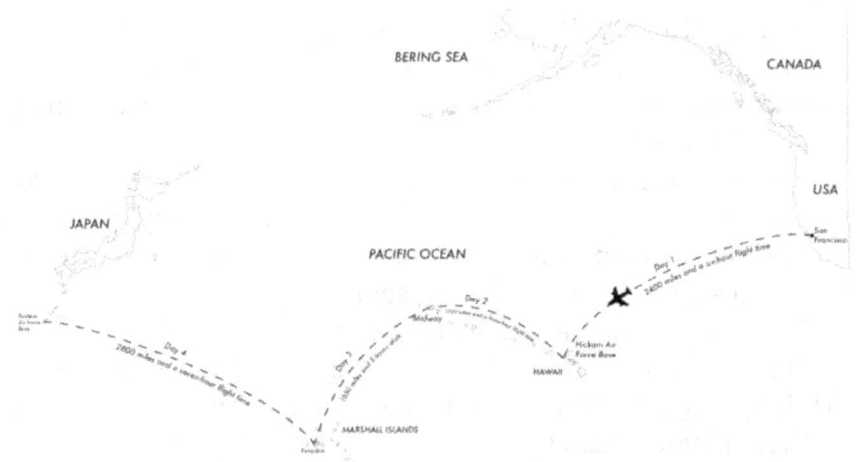

Wind over the Pacific was not bad, and the six-hour flight stayed smooth, mostly. We caught the tail end of a rain squall enroute but arrived at Hickham AFB. It seemed gorgeous from the air, and I looked forward to being on the ground. Most of the scars from the Pearl Harbor attack were gone: painted over, planted over or rebuilt.

They put us up in the Royal Hawaiian Hotel for our layover day. Terraces outside each room let in the warm breeze and fragrant smells of the hotel gardens. Our two flights met as agreed in the hotel bar. Twins Two had also enjoyed a safe and easy flight over.

After our full day of rest, our planes waited, gassed and ready to go. Back in the air at 0800, we were on the beam and headed for Midway Island, a short three-hour hop.

As we flew, I appreciated details right there in the cockpit. A cozy space, for sure, though a bigger body might find it cramped. My seat had fold-down armrests, and they fixed a cup holder to the right corner of the instrument panel. I found a knob that controlled cockpit hot air flow from the Allison engine. The heater control was below the dashboard and the vent down by my left foot.

The only mystery: an ashtray. Yes, an ashtray. Maybe it's just me, but here I am surrounded by hundreds of gallons of 145-

octane aviation fuel. As gas tanks empty, fumes increase. So, what could go wrong having a smoke with gas fumes and compressed oxygen for my mask, all in a tiny space? I didn't want to find out.

Banducci turned out to love humor. Whether or not I asked, he always had a joke of the day. "After mass one day, this priest notices one old woman still sitting alone in the church. He goes over and says, 'Hello Maria, you seem sad.'

"'Father, my Joe passed away last night.'

"'I'm so sorry. Now, I know Joe had his problems, the drinking, the gambling. Maria, you were a saint.'

"'Thank you, Father.'

"'Tell me, did he have any last words?'

"'Yes, Father, he said, 'Maria put the gun down.'"

I laughed at the joke and Bianucci's deadpan delivery.

* * * *

A crosswind buffeted us as we landed at Midway Island. Every pilot knew about the Navy pilots who'd stopped the Japanese advance into these same waters. I didn't want to fly an old Douglas Dauntless, but I admired the men who had.

Twins One taxied to a stop at three adjoining hard stands. Our brother flight, Twins Two, was not far behind.

"Twins Two leader, this is Williams. We are on the ground and proceeding to Ops to check in, roger?"

"Roger that."

"We'll probably see you at Ops, but if not, we'll be at the O Club bar at 1900 and will look for you there."

"Roger that. Drink slow please. Out."

Midway Island, small but essential because of its position, had no other apparent redeeming features. Here was another candidate for insertion of an enema tube.

I checked with Walt Williams if we would push on or overnight there. He decided we'd stay the night. With the fueling time, double-checking our planes and a meal, doing the next five-hour leg to Kwajalein immediately would pose needless risks. But we'd skip the one-day layover since we'd only been three hours in the air.

With a night's sleep and fresh hot coffee in my thermos, the five hours to Kwajalein passed uneventfully. Banducci and I shared stories about home. He turned out to be a recreational cook.

"I learned at my mother's knee, back home in McAlester, Oklahoma. Simple things are best. Let the ingredients speak. A simple polenta with a good olive oil, rabbit stew or Osso Bucco cooked for six hours in red sauce. Beautiful!"

The ride to Kwajalein was bumpy and uncomfortable but not worrisome. "Rico, remind me to check the shock absorbers on this thing when we get on the ground."

"You got it, Red."

The local equivalent of the Royal Hawaiian was a Quonset hut, but the beer in the all-ratings club was cold. The only foliage was palm trees, and the only wildlife, land crabs. Happily, we would leave at 0800 the next morning, again skipping the allowed a one-day layover. Seven hours flying to Okinawa tomorrow and our travels would be done, for now.

* * * *

Two hours into our flight, Banducci began humming to himself, but our open mic shared it with me and the entire flight. Then he started singing.

"Ay, ay, ay, ay, Canta y no llores."

I recognized the tune as "Cielito Lindo," an old Mexican folk song well known back in the states.

"Ay, ay, ay, ay, they always serve kim chi in Pusan." The improvisation made me smile.

"And now here is an Italian folk song for you guys."

Then Walt Williams' voice came over our mics. "Red, if Rico starts singing again, prepare to bail out. Rico, my guns are loaded. If you sing anymore, I'll have to shoot you down. Sorry Red, but I have no choice. For the good of the flight."

We passed through rain squalls about once per hour. Our training had included elementary meteorology, so I knew enough to avoid clouds that potentially held lightning or rough winds.

Suddenly, my left calf cramped. The pain was immediate and unrelenting. Confined in this narrow space, 8,000 feet above the Pacific, I tried hard not to scream. It hurt that bad, but screams would interfere with my five other friends flying along with me. I reached down and massaged my calf, but it did no good. I couldn't stand, but I hoisted my butt from the seat and rotated my pelvis to the right. Could I find some position, some contortion that gave me some relief?

"Rico, take over the controls. I've got a leg cramp, and it's bad." I saw his head turn to face me and a nod of agreement.

God almighty, this hurt, and no space, no position helped. I thought I was about to pass out. My eyes watered, my forehead wrinkled, as I did my best to suffer in silence. Oh man, it hurt. I reached my thermos of water and drank. Maybe I was dehydrated? But drinking didn't help.

I continued to massage with my right hand. Could I reach and unlace my boot? Something, anything, was worth trying as the pain ran up my leg and infected my mind and my body. Nothing else but ending the pain mattered.

I couldn't unlace the boot with my one hand, however hard I tried. But I bent over enough to grab the toe of my boot and pull it toward me, forcing my foot to bend and stretch the knotted calf muscle. The cramp eased slowly but eased nonetheless. Finally, the pain vanished. I was spent. All I did was slump back into my seat and close my eyes. Flying, living or dying mattered not, as long as the pain was gone.

When I tried to use my hands, they still shook. I'm not proud to say that I couldn't keep the relief tube funnel steady, and I pissed all over my leg. The rest if the way to Okinawa, my simple prayer was, "Kill me, but don't let the cramp return."

21. Okinawa, May 1, 1950

Kadena AFB was in the middle of Okinawa. The scars of war were still visible on the land not yet reclaimed by thick foliage. Here and there, the remains of vehicles or fighting positions still peeked out from the advancing green carpet.

With white sand beaches and clear blue water, this would be a hell of a nice place if not for the scourge of war. Our series of runways, hangars and buildings did nothing to improve the look of the island. We just covered over what had gone before.

Happy as I was to be on the ground, my first stop after checking into squadron and quarters would be with a flight surgeon. The cramp I'd just suffered might have killed us if it happened in combat. If it had happened in a single-seat jet, I'd be dead now.

A flight surgeon had to act on anything he saw or heard that put pilots, planes, or operational capability at risk. Rico assured me he had kept silent about my cramp. Even though I could hide the event for now, I wouldn't do that. I went to see the Flight surgeon the following day.

"Lieutenant Black, what can I do for you?"

I laid out an unedited, unvarnished description of what had happened.

"And you would like me to prescribe a solution to your problem."

I responded, "Yes sir."

Questions and answers followed, as he filled in details of the picture I'd painted. He leaned back in his desk chair and summarized. "So, you made a series of long flights, for the first time in the very confined cockpit of a fighter plane. Except for training flights, your prior experience was in a bomber crew. You consumed half a thermos of coffee during the flight from Kwajalein. Correct?"

I acknowledged he was correct on all accounts.

"I have a probable solution for you to try out. You need to stay well hydrated, both before and during your flight. Avoid caffeine because it is a diuretic and dehydrates you. Understood?"

I nodded.

"Cramps are also related to low blood magnesium and potassium. Go heavy on green leafy vegetables, cereals and fruits. Can you do that?"

My answer was, "Probably."

"Since all your airtime is going to be in the F-82, our long-range heavy fighter and one hell of an aircraft, I'll prescribe a vitamin supplement. That should do the job. Come back if the problem returns," and he stood, signaling our meeting had concluded.

"One more thing Doc. I have bad dreams. Have you got anything that can help me turn them off?" I left with a prescription for sleeping pills to try.

Banducci and I had gotten close. Shared danger will do that. He had his own unwanted dreams.

"Red, mine are just silent, still pictures of things I can't unsee, no matter how hard I try. The pictures hurt. Some make me mad. Some make me ashamed."

I understood.

"Sometimes I think it would be better to be dead. Then I wouldn't hurt anymore." Then perhaps thinking he might alarm me, Rico continued. "Don't worry, if I ever decide to pull the plug and go to the big vineyard in the sky, I won't be taking anyone else along."

I could only nod my understanding.

I shared what I'd learned with Banducci about the cramps and the pills. I swore off coffee before and during patrols. The two of us agreed, since our plane had dual controls, only one of us on any day would use go pills. This strategy kept us safe, with no risk of getting hooked on the little white pills.

Our squadron assignment changed from the 51st to the 68th (All Weather) Squadron, that only flew the F-82 night fighters. I went aloft every night to get accustomed to flying in darkness. Good idea.

"Rico, are you seeing the same exhaust flames I'm seeing over here? We look like a fire-breathing dragon. I'm going to ask our crew chief if he can extend the flame suppressors."

"Same problem over on my right. They advertise our presence and flight path. Kind of like an enormous neon sign, 'shoot here'."

Thus began our 'punch list' of things to fix or change so we could stay alive.

Discovery number two came three nights later during live fire practice. Armed to the teeth with a full load of 25 High-Velocity Aircraft Rockets, we lifted off. "I want to see how she handles a barrage firing of the HVARs. If you have us low to the ground, I don't want to tip, dip or buck when we fire these puppies." So, from a safe altitude, I lit off the full salvo.

"Holy shit, I'm blind. Rico, my night vision is gone, man. All I'm seeing is a giant yellow blur. Take the controls."

Lucky for us, Banducci's eyes had been focused on the green of the radar screen. "I'm okay, Red. I'll drive for a while."

I waited for the afterimage to go, vowing never to fire more than one HVAR from each under-wing rack at the same time. Another lesson learned.

I found that the sleeping pills did knock me out. No dreams at all. But I never woke up rested and this was affecting my flying, so I dumped the pills.

I hate surprises, so our last lesson was about dropping napalm. Part of what gave us such great range was an ability to carry two underwing 175-gallon auxiliary tanks. Full of gas, they gave me a range of 3,500 miles. Full of napalm, they gave us another card to play.

"I'm dropping the napalm in three, two, one; tanks away," and our plane shuddered. "Rico, what the hell was that?"

He had no clue, but something had rocked the ship the moment I release the two tanks.

Back on the ground, we did a walk-around and realized what had happened. On both wings, the ailerons, which give us the ability to roll, were scarred and bent. The napalm tanks must have flipped back instead of dropping straight away. I shared the experience with the S-4 Supply Officer, our ground crew chief, and the other air crews. They needed to know, and we needed a solution. The best advice was to reduce airspeed as much as possible before dropping. Oh, and hope for the best!

* * * *

Our six aircrews received an initial situation briefing from the squadron's S-2 officer, someone I'd be dealing with a lot. The S-2 section of squadron administration collected data on enemy movements, strengths and deployment. They also were our source for radio codes and maps. What we heard darkened my mental picture of what we'd just flown into.

We were watching a guerilla war being used by Joe Stalin to paint the rest of Asia red. Our CIA believed with the fall of Nationalist China, our withdrawal of troops from Korea, and Russia having the bomb, Stalin felt the time was right to invade the South. A hot war could break out at any time. Stalin had been supplying weapons, training, and money to North Korea. We knew war was coming, but when? How soon?

The Air Force was scrounging fighter planes from all over the world. Sadly, their cupboard was bare in what we now needed. Winding down from World War Two and scrapping planes might now be a problem. On hand or enroute were a paltry 145 F-51s, 90 F-82 fighters and a handful of B-26s. Our new jets, for all their speed and promise, were comparatively short-range air-to-air fighters.

22. War, 1950

On June 25, 1950, the North Koreans sent 10 Divisions, about 200,000 men, across the 38th parallel. In three days' time, South Korean President Rhee fled the capitol, Seoul, and the city fell to the communists.

On June 27th, five F-82s were providing top cover for our transport planes evacuating civilians from Seoul. They intercepted a flight of enemy fighters sent to attack the transports. Our F-82's fought off the enemy planes and got the first air-to-air kill in the war.

On June 30, 1950, the first American ground troops arrived in Osan, Korea. Their purpose was to blunt the North Korean advance. Our fight for Osan lasted seven hours before our badly mauled force retreated south. In July 1950, United Nations forces joined us in the fight. Defeat after defeat followed as we fell back toward the port of Pusan.

Our final foothold on the Korean peninsula continued to shrink through the month of August. Finally, the north retreated after our amphibious landing at Incheon in September 1950. In October 1950, China entered the war, and the first MiG 15 fighter jets began attacking from their safe haven across the Yalu River in China.

What kept us on Korean soil before the Incheon landing was our airpower. Navy jets flew off carriers, but stopping the North's ground advance was the work of the last propeller planes. Why? Because we were there and that was what we had.

Here's the deal with our Twin Mustangs in 1950. North American stopped building these babies in 1949. Of the 270 ever built, only about 200 were still around and 110 of these belonged to SAC for bomber protection.

Most of the bigwigs back in the 'Puzzle Palace,' as we referred to our command headquarters, believed that bombers won the last war. Now, these guys never flew in a bomber, but they had the numbers and they were smart. Just ask them. Anyway, SAC, our bomber Mafia, got the first call on our only long-range fighter plane capable of escorting bombers to Russia and back. Twelve fighter squadrons flew F-82s and only three of them were our night fighters in Korea.

Our three squadrons had to compete for an ever-dwindling supply of spare parts. Flying from 30 minutes after dark until 30 minutes before sunrise took a heavy toll on our planes. Now, I'm almost done with my bitching here, so bear with me. The radar dongs hanging down from our planes were fragile and time-consuming to repair. Bottom line: on any day, 40 percent of our aircraft were sidelined. Rico and I flew whatever plane wasn't getting repaired or waiting to get repaired.

23. We Shoot, August 1950 Above the Pusan Perimeter

The battle to save our foothold at Pusan had started. North Koreans were roaring south. Rico and I still were flying our original plane. Tonight, we had a blind date: 20 of us and an equal number of B-26 Douglas Invaders. I knew the Invader, and it was the only ground attack plane more fearsome than our F-82s.

We rendezvoused off the coast and headed inland over Pusan, on the hunt for anything and everything. Walt Williams was the A Flight leader of five Twins. He would pick our targets and set the attack plan.

"A Flight, we've got a truck convoy ahead," Walt's voice sounded in our ears. "Follow me in and then break right and come back around. Acknowledge," and we did. I was third in the attack formation.

"Rico, I've got the stick and the guns. You've got the HVARs." Because of our lessons learned, Rico would fire one HVAR from each underwing rack at each burst.

We swooped to 100 feet above the trucks. "I'm going in fast and out quick. This low, they'll be shooting at us with rifles and submachine guns."

Troops and truck drivers ran from their vehicles. Windshields shattered, and gas tanks exploded into fireballs. As the convoy disintegrated and troops ran for cover, I could hear an occasional bullet ping on our metal. That quick, we were past the convoy and coming around for a second bite. I heard our radio click inside my helmet. It was Walt.

"Twin 2, you and I are going to lay down suppressing fire on those small arms. I'll take left. You've got the right. Twins 3 and 4, hit anything not already burning. Twin 5, stay in top cover."

"Rico, same drill. Let's go kill some commies!" Being careful not to stare into the flames, we made our second run. I set my sights on a truck-mounted .50 caliber machine gun. His shots at me came like a flaming finger of red tracer rounds. I dipped down to 50 feet and wagged my wings right, then left. If he wanted to shoot us, he'd better be good. And he was.

In one split second a volley of bullets stitched a line over the radar pod and center boom, rattling our plane.

But we were better, and our six Browning .50 calibers carved up the truck and the shooter as we zoomed past. Behind us lay probably 100 flaming trucks and equal number or more of dead men.

"A flight, how are you doing back there? Anyone hit?" When the answers came back, we were all still good. "Next stop is their front line. The B-26 Invaders hit the artillery on the ridge line and now we are going to hit the troops positioned in front. One-two will fan out right, four-five, fan left. Red, you and Rico are our center. First run, guns and HVAR's. Second pass, we hit them with the napalm: same attack formation. Questions?" None came.

"Follow me around and in. Good luck."

I watched the spacing between Walt's plane and our number two. I moved in on their left and saw my two pals spaced out beside me. While I listened for our 'go' signal, my adrenaline level hit a new high.

We started our angle of attack, as an invisible scythe blade swinging in the dark. The sounds and flames of the B-26's cannon attacks marked our target. Our 30 combined machine guns all opened up at once with a hot and deadly rain against their trenches and sandbags. Our first fast pass caught their troops by surprise. Our return would not.

Around we came, holding our line as tracer bullets reached up to greet us. The jellied napalm bombs would splash ahead of their impact point. Our speed and guns answering their fire were our only protection. "Ready, drop on my mark and climb to beat hell, then follow me back to the coast and home. "

Drop-drop-drop filled my head as time stretched and the bullets rising to meet us slowed.

"DROP-DROP!" and we did, and just a second later I pointed our two props toward the sky. Once away, we shifted back to our normal 'V' formation and followed our flight leader around from high above. A two-hundred-yard wall of flame blazed behind us as we headed home.

Five hours after departing Kadena, we were back on the ground. Rico and I did a walk around our plane. Half a dozen holes pocked her metal and, as expected, scratches marked our ailerons from the napalm drops. The enemy machine gunner who died at his gun had left his mark. Our radar pod took four hits. The line of .50 caliber punctures continued up through the center boom that separated our twin cockpits. But we'd killed a lot of men who wanted to kill us and we'd come back unharmed.

24. Pilot Down

I have some good news and some bad news," the Nazi guard said to the camp inmate. "The good news is that you are going to a better place. Beautiful women, fine food and vintage wine will surround you. The bad news is you're going as a lampshade."

So it was for me that month in Korea: some good news and some bad. The good news was my promotion to captain came through, so I would pin on new silver bars. Now for the bad news. In October, General McArthur finally got his wish, and UN forces crossed above the 38th parallel and headed for the Yalu River at the Chinese border. What could go wrong?

We had some dedicated flight paths. Navy night fighters flying off carriers covered some patrol routes along the Korean coast. Our squadrons covered others. But what we did the most and best was interdiction patrols and top cover for air rescues.

I'd seen for myself how the quality of German pilots declined as the war went on. It's simple. It takes more time to train pilots than it does to build planes. In 1950, our downed pilots were supposed to 'walk out' if they crashed. The same for Navy flyers. They were told to head for the coast and signal for a 'Downed Flyer' rescue boat pickup. Doing top cover for the Air Force Air Rescue Service or the Navy was a carefully orchestrated ballet of coordination.

Air Force and Navy air controllers alerted one or both of the air rescue services when one of their planes went down. Was the pilot wounded? His wingman stayed over the crash site for as long as he could, hopefully until a replacement covered for him and a helicopter arrived.

The downed flyer call went out immediately to our fighter group. Our group leader then assigned missions based on where the pilot was thought to have gone down. The location information was sent to the Sikorsky Dragonfly helicopters on the nearest carrier or at the closest Air Force Air Rescue Squadron.

Interdiction patrol over Korea was our nightly job. We soon banished the Chinese, Russians, and North Koreans from the skies below the 38th parallel. Along the Yalu River was MiG Alley. Up there, the MiG 15s ventured out to pick fights with our jets. We learned about the traps they set and tricks they used to lure our flights into ambushes. MiG Alley made the dangerous pilot rescues even more difficult.

Interdiction patrols over Korea were our daily job. The enemy began moving their troops and supplies at night. Our night fighter Twin Mustangs had the radar to find targets. Sometimes friendly units on the ground cued us to enemy movements.

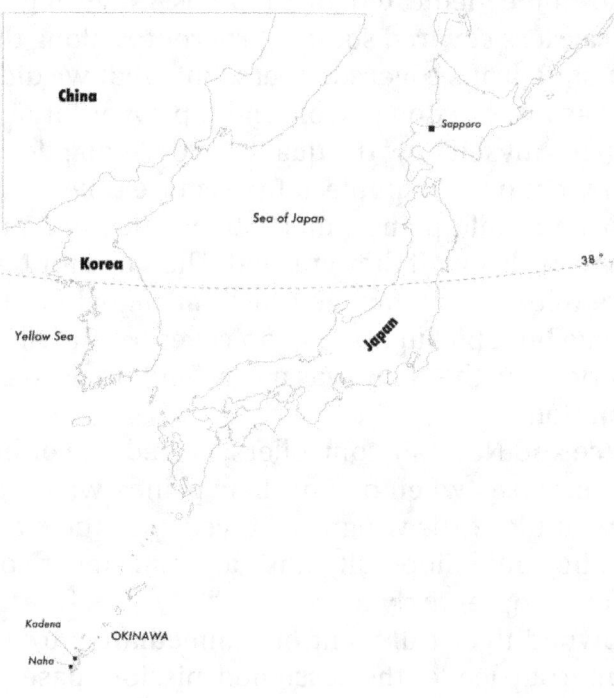

After Pusan, we flew patrol over the Yellow Sea along the west coast of Korea. So far, we'd met no intruders from the air.

Our station off Changyou, North Korea, put us on call to swoop in and shoot the shit out of any enemy columns or formations that cropped up.

Most every night we provided top cover for a downed flyer. Because bad news doesn't get any better with time, I'll give you the rest now; sorry. Only about one in ten downed flyers got rescued. But we came every time anyway because our guys had to know someone was coming.

* * * *

"Gabriel station, do you copy?"

I snapped my mask back to my helmet and answered.

"Gabriel, we have an F-51 pilot who bailed from his crippled bird in your zone. The pilot had been strafing enemy positions, so his pickup location is hot. His wingman has only 15 minutes more as cover. Coordinates are as follows," and they transmitted map references. "We have an H-5 helo inbound, 50 minutes out. Can you provide top cover?"

"Heard, and on our way," I replied. "Rico, did you catch all that?"

"Got it. I'm figuring our course change now." I waited and with his usual efficiency Banducci called out the heading for our new course. I put the Allisons up to full power, and we headed to the pilot at 460 miles per hour. I was now flying our third Twin Mustang, as numbers one and two were waiting for replacement parts.

I couldn't shake my recollection and mental images from our last four pilot rescue attempts. The images of dead flyers haunted my dreams. We'd arrived too late. No less maddening were remembrances of pilots shot dead before my eyes. It was cold comfort to me that I'd killed the killers, but too late. The memories were perhaps my penance for hesitating or not pushing hard enough. I hoped they were purgatory and not my personal hell.

Pilots were high-value captures for the commies. They were worth more in prisoner trades. But their most sinister use was for worldwide propaganda. Everyone has a breaking point. After sufficient abuse and torture, their coerced confessions to targeting civilians or dropping 'germ bombs' helped display their aggression to the eyes of the world.

"Red, we should be over our guy in about one minute. Watch for his signal." Pilots who crashed with their planes might call us in via relayed radio messages.

This guy, on the ground alone and who-knows-where from the crash site, didn't have that luxury. He had a flashlight, flares and a signaling mirror, useless of course now at night. He had an emergency radio to call for help, and lucky for him, he was an Air Force flyer. Navy and Marine airborne radio equipment were not linked to Air Force equipment. Their flyers had to have calls for Air Force cover relayed through base stations. Who knows why?

We had an almost-full moon and a cloudless sky going for us, sort of. Good news, bad news. We could see him more easily, but so could the commies.

"I got him; flashlight at our two o'clock."

Training my eyes on Rico's spot, I cut our speed back, dropped to 1,000 feet and wagged our wings, letting the pilot know we'd seen his signal. I began a slow, tight circle overhead.

"Rico, do you see his wingman?"

"Negative," he replied. "Try to get an ETA for the helo. I'll scout for bad guys on the ground." We'd been 20 minutes getting overhead. If the enemy had seen the wingman's departure, they would have moved in for a kill or capture.

"Helo is 30 out." I dropped to 500 feet for a better chance of seeing any approaching enemy. I could see the shapes of scattered trees in the distance, but the moonlight showed our downed pilot had nothing more than knee-high scrub for cover.

And I found them. Squad-sized groups of troops, their dull brown quilted uniforms almost invisible against the ground, but their movement betrayed them. "Rico, I've got troops at our 12 o'clock. I'm going in. Give those boys a couple of HVARS and I'll give em' a taste of the Brownings."

I came around and locked in on them from 100 feet. The glow of the two rockets momentarily illuminated our plane against the sky. Six Browning machine guns steadily spit hot metal. I watched as our .50 caliber bullets stitched paths up to and on through their approaching groups. The earth kicked up when hit and bodies crumpled or exploded when one or more machine gun rounds struck.

I saw muzzle flashes from their return fire and heard communist bullets hit our plane. My head jerked left when one bullet struck a glancing blow to my canopy, less than one foot from my face. I banked right to attack a second group of troops moving toward our pilot. "Rico, here we go, round two. Same deal." *We've got to cover that poor bastard. That could be me,* was the only thought that filled my mind. The feeling, even beyond the bounds of thought, only grew. I hated those men on the ground, just as surely and as irrationally as they hated me.

At one hundred feet, enemy faces were almost clear. Not clear enough to register surprise, pain or anger, as our rockets and bullets sliced into them. They shot back as we shot, perhaps taking some comfort in standing their ground and bravely defying the fire-spouting Valkyrie charging them from above. Seeing the enemy standing tall in the face of our attack brought forth my admiration, which momentarily cut through my hate. I respected a fellow warrior.

I took the plane back up to 1,000 feet and resumed my tight circle above the pilot, huddled below with only a .45 pistol for protection. "Rico, any damage over there?" I asked, eyes now on my friend in the right-hand seat.

"Nope."

"Check on the helo." My eyes went back to the moonlit ground, as I search below for other enemy soldiers inching closer to our pilot. I saw a single soldier on the advance and angled us down firing our guns. Now I scanned my instrument panel and checked the small counters, showing how many rounds left for each of my six guns. Rico had the same array inside his cockpit, and my count would match his, since I'd controlled and fired all six of our machine guns. Two hundred rounds per gun were still on board, half of what our armorers had loaded.

"Red, they're six out. They're taking small arms fire. Should I check if they want us to swing off and cover them?"

"No, we stay here. I have a debt to the 51 pilots. They never left me, not once, and I will not leave one of them now. The helo is less than five out. Our ground is clear. You can either turn on our landing light or put an HVAR straight down to give them a beacon in."

"Yeah, good idea. I'll switch on the lights and get as close to our man as we can."

From our top cover at 1,000 feet, I took us up to 3,000 feet. The Sikorsky Dragon Fly could hover in below us with no danger of a mid-air collision. First, I saw his lights in the night sky. Then, even above our propeller noise, I heard the beat of their rotors as they headed straight in. The pilot's flashlight beam signaled them from the ground.

"Rico, watch out for commies. They may have held back, hoping to get a helo and a pilot at once." From reports of other pilots, I knew the commies were evil but not dumb. They learned and adapted their methods into new tricks. We only learned about a new ploy from someone who'd fallen into one of their traps and survived.

Rico and I watched as the Dragon Fly touched down just long enough for the Mustang pilot to climb aboard. When the helo lifted off, I told Rico, "Tell him we'll ride shotgun for them back to Seoul." The capitol was back in our hands, for the moment at least.

Each time small arms fire rose from below, we swooped down from our slow circle of top cover and carpeted the ground with bullets. The helo made it back safe. We headed for the friendly skies along the Korean West coast, with its cover of Navy jets.

25. Late October 1950

"Rico, have you heard the latest? When the Marines captured Pyongyang, the North capitol, they found the bodies of 75 GIs who had been executed."

Banducci shook his head, spitting out "dirty bastards."

It was almost two years since the last Twin Mustang had rolled out of the factory in Southern California. They had produced no spare parts since then. The 68th was down to nine operational planes. Command hoped that the F-94 Starfire jets would arrive soon. In the meantime, we were it for available night fighters.

"What did operations say, Red? What's on deck for us?"

"We are going back on night coast patrol duty. Ours are the only planes with the legs to go the distance and stay on station for the night. Exciting huh, Rico?"

"Yeah, just another shitty day in paradise, Red."

* * * *

Captain Frank Mills lost an air battle with two MiG 15s and went down over the rugged T'aebaek Mountains. Using his emergency radio, Mills advised that his leg got broken in the crash. The Air Force Air Rescue Service, alerted to the crash, answered the call. Mills' wingman had escaped the ambush and relayed coordinates for the crash site.

"Captain, this is air rescue. We're arranging extraction for you now, sir. Hang in there." Mills' transmission was weak. Distance, damage to the radio or a low battery, it didn't matter. Air rescue contacted the 68th Lightning Lancers at Kadena. We got the radio call from squadron HQ as we cruised the Korean coast.

"Gabriel Station, this is Kadena HQ." Rico was busy staring at the green of his radar screen and the call arrived in my helmet. "Go ahead, Kadena," I replied.

"We've got a 51 down in your zone, in the T'aebaeks, north of the 38th. Grid reference for crash site is as follows."

I copied down two map coordinates.

"Air Rescue has his radio squawk, but only weakly. Capt. Frank Mills. His squawk is on…" and they provided the emergency radio frequency. "Make contact, locate the crash site and provide cover." They gave me the radio contact for their rescue helo. "Air Rescue, Team Bravo, out,"

"Roger, Kadena." I tapped our intercom switch, alerting Rico to expect me in his ear. "Hey Rico, we've got a job. F-51 down. I've got his radio squawk. I'm going to raise him. We're heading northeast for now. Here are the crash coordinates on our map grid."

"I got ya, Red. I will switch to ground radar as soon as we have the coast in sight."

* * * *

"Fifty-one down, fifty-one down, this is Gabriel station. Do you copy?" I waited for a comeback response, if our pilot was alive and not captured by the commies.

"Gabriel station, this is Mustang 6. I've got your copy. I read you five by five."

At his response, I keyed our intercom, "Rico, I've got him. Switch to ground radar. Alert Kadena that we've made contact. They'll relay to Air Rescue. Oh, and try to get an ETA on the helo."

"Six, this is Red. What is your condition? One broken leg?"

Mustang Six confirmed the injury and described the conditions on the ground. He was down between two mountains. There was snow on the ground. He'd stayed at the crash site.

"Any bad guys in sight?"

Fortunately, the enemy hadn't approached yet.

"Mustang Six, we will be overhead in 20. You'll hear us before you see us. Give me a heads up when you've got us."

"Red, rescue from Seoul is 30 out. They have an escort of two 51s."

I passed the news to the downed pilot as I maxed the Allisons and headed into the T'aebaeks. "Rico, stay sharp and save me from putting us into a mountain." We had 15 minutes more to go.

"Mustang Six, what's your unit?"

His answer was the 67th Fighter Squadron. "My name is Frank."

I worked to keep him awake as his voice faded in and out, possibly because of shock. I remembered my cramp and how the pain filled my senses. We shared family legends as the minutes inched by.

"So, baseball or football. What's your game?" I asked.

Frank hailed from Cleveland and was an Indians fan. "You relax and concentrate on listening for us. The same engine sound as from your 51. Give me a squawk when you hear us or if you see any bad guys."

We were 10 minutes out, according to Rico's figuring. The rescue helo was still inbound, 20 minutes out. We flew on through the night as I dropped altitude and slowed my airspeed. Five minutes or fewer to Frank.

"Red, I've got the crash site on my radar. Two o'clock and two miles ahead. Watch the mountains. The T'aebaeks go seven to nine thousand feet." I acknowledged Rico's news. I'd have to keep in a tight circle. The aluminum of the downed F-51 reflected moonlight. Frank was several hundred feet up the right-hand slope of the notch between mountain peaks.

"Frank, we've got you. Your ride is only five minutes out." His only response was a single word, "Right."

"Listen brother, we'll have you back at base, then you'll be on your way to Japan. I'll let you know when I'm in Cleveland and we'll take in an Indians game."

Then I picked up a change in his voice, but what and why?

"Brownie, I'm a football fan. Make it a Cleveland Lions game and the beers are on me."

What the hell? His answers weren't lining up. He'd changed my name, his favorite sport and favorite team. But why?

"Frank, hey, I'm sorry. Remind me which unit are you with?" I knew the answer. Would I get it back correctly from the man on the ground?

"651st Flying Turkeys." The helo was only minutes from touching down. Either something wasn't right, or Frank's mind had succumbed to shock. I needed to know, before the five-man air rescue crew landed.

"Yeah, that's right, sorry. Hey, I remember you told me you loved golf. Think you could teach me?"

"Buddy, I'm afraid you should write me off. All I can do is try to keep you out of a sand "TRAP," and he shouted the keyword. A gun to his head? A knife to his throat? I'd never know. But I pulled up and warned off the helo. Frank Mills just gave his life to save the seven of us.

* * * *

My instinct was to shoot the shit out of the crash site, killing anyone on the ground, but I didn't. Frank Mills' only faint hope was to survive until a prisoner exchange. Then the North Koreans sprang the rest of their trap.

"Red, we've got two MiGs inbound, coming down the slot from the north." We were not a match for the two jets, and neither were our two F-51s. I banked hard left, heading for the coast, and the helo turned back, with the covering F-51s lagging as rear guards in case of attack. The pair of MiGs split up, one following the helo and the other close on my tail. I couldn't outrun the jet, so it was fight or die escaping.

"Rico, jettison the radar dong. When I turn, I'm shooting, and I want you to give him the full volley of HVARS. I need to scare or blind that son of a bitch long enough for us to get away," and I paused. "I'm going to be blinded by the HVAR blasts, so close your eyes the instant you shoot." Another pause. "I'm going to need your help in flying this thing. OK?"

"Do it." And I started a tight bank, hoping to get back around to face our foe before he cut loose with his guns and cannons.

We made it around. The MiG was still closing. I angled our nose up slightly to better place our volley of 25 HVARs. "Now!" and we both fired. I had to keep my eyes open to avoid colliding with the MiG. As expected, the blazing glow of 25 HVARs streaking through the night sky blinded my eyes like a hundred flash bulbs.

As we fired, he fired. Blinded or bluffed by our head-on attack, his 37-millimeter cannon fire went wide. But machine-gun bullets stitched across my left wing and canopy. His fire hit one of the aluminum braces that supported my front windshield. Hot metal shards pierced my cheek and torso, narrowly missing my eyes. Blood poured down my cheeks and my eyes teared up. I felt the blast of cold air that now rushed into the cockpit.

"Rico, I'm hit. You are my eyes, man. What's the MiG doing?"

"He must really love his wife and kids. He's broken off and is heading back north. We did it!"

"Keep level and direct. Get us to coast and then south to Kadena." Our plane had dual flight controls from the second seat. We had three hours in the air ahead of us.

I needed to stay awake even if I couldn't see to fly. I closed my eyes, hoping to speed the departure of the afterimages from the rocket blasts. I snapped on my mask and dropped the helmet's eye shield. It made it harder not to fall asleep. I guess Rico monitored me, seven feet off to his left. Whenever my head dropped, his voice was there in my ears, keeping me awake.

"Red, did I tell you about the former Kamikaze pilot I met in Japan?" There was no pausing for me to answer. This was therapy, not comedy.

"The squadron commander briefs his Kamikaze flight about crashing into American ships. So, this guy raises his hand.

"'We crash our planes into the ship. Blow up ship and my plane?'

"'Hai,' says the briefer.

"Our pilot nods. 'Ah so, you crazy son of a bitch,' and he walked out of the briefing." Rico paused and checked if my head was still up. "After the war, this guy is a celebrity. They even name a dish after him. Chicken Teriyaki."

One joke later, after the divorce of Mickey and Minnie Mouse (not because she was crazy but because she was fucking Goofy), I'd come around. The blood had stopped flowing and dried into what felt like stripes down my cheeks. My vision was better as the afterimage faded. "How much longer back to Kadena? I can't read my watch."

"About 30 minutes more. The helo and 51s made it back safe, so we did a good day's work. And lived to tell about it."

"Good, and thanks for checking." I tried my vison. "Rico, can you land this puppy?"

"It's been a hell of a long time since I've landed anything, but hey, it's like riding a bicycle, right, Red? I'll call Kadena tower and have them roll out fire and rescue, just in case."

"We're in this together, so take us in."

Rico's landing was something of a shit show, but we walked away. Medics were there along with the fire crew. They took me out and drove off to the base clinic.

"Captain, I'm taking you off the flight roster because of your line of duty injury," said our Flight Surgeon. "I'm recommending you see an ophthalmologist at the 343rd General Hospital in Tokyo. I can see some retinal damage, but a specialist is what you need."

My cheeks and chest wounds had shrapnel removed, and I kept the aluminum splinters as souvenirs. Three days later I was on a C-47 plane, bound for Tokyo.

Before leaving, I got together with Rico and filled him in. With another F-82 out of service, the 68th was down to five planes. Perhaps, as Napoleon said, "An Army marches on its stomach." Did anyone say that an Air Force flies on its spare parts? It does.

With me away, Banducci was a free man for the moment, if being in uniform on Okinawa qualifies as being free. At least he was at liberty.

It ended up being almost a month for me to get an appointment, be seen, tested for all kinds of visual parameters and returned to flight status. In all that time, I never met Chicken Teriyaki, but I celebrated his dish.

The doc diagnosed that I had a torn cornea and a small retinal bleed. Corneas heal fast; retinas do not, but they do heal. I'd be getting treated for some months to have my right eye fully recovered. While I was off flying status, the Air Force decided to fill my time with non-flying duties as Operations Officer for the 4th Fighter Squadron at Naha, Okinawa.

And in my dreams, I'd added mental images of Frank Mills, surrounded by his Korean captors, watching us fly off.

26. The Habu and the Mongoose

As its number two man, I ran the day-to-day operations of the squadron. Along with the promotion to Operations Officer came "Other duties as assigned." As soon as I was returned to flying status, they assigned me as flight instructor for the B-26 Invaders. This 'other duty,' I liked. Those planes are beasts and the best ground attack plane we've produced. Besides, the job would get me back in the air and out from behind a desk. It also kept me qualified on the B-26. That might come in handy if our inventory of F-82 night-fighters continued to decline.

The rest of the other duty package included being in charge of the service club. Naha was not big enough to rate separate Officers and Enlisted clubs. My job was strictly oversight: making sure government funds were spent on the club and not stolen. Our first addition to the bar stock was my Martell's Cognac. I wanted the club to be unique, memorable and classy.

"Captain Black, I've got something for you to try," said Koshi, the bar manager. "Awamori, Okinawan rice whisky. Nice. This is our local spirit since the 15th century."

"I'm game."

He poured a sample. "We drink it over ice and sometimes with just a splash of water."

I smelled, then sipped. "Hmm, like Saki, but stronger," I said. "Do you stock this stuff?"

Not yet, but Koshi wanted to bring it in.

"All right, try it. I'm all for supporting the island. Are there any other special Okinawan things you think might be popular?"

He thought about it for less than a minute. "Habu and mongoose fights."

I needed to be educated about Habu, which are pit vipers colored in dark bands over gray, red, or yellow bodies. "How big are these things?"

"Four to five feet average, but up to nine feet long."

"Poisonous?"

"Oh yes, like a Cobra."

"So, a mongoose is kind of like a weasel? I've never seen one. California is not mongoose country."

"Yes, a big weasel, very fast, and they hate snakes. Even better, they eat snakes."

"So where would we get a habu?"

"No problem, boss. At the market in the village or we can go out behind the club tonight and catch one right here." I didn't like the sound of that.

"Snakes on base, huh?"

"Okinawa is lousy with them. That is why we brought in the mongoose. Snake patrol!"

"Okay, okay, so who wins, the habu or the mongoose?"

"Hmm, usually the mongoose, maybe seven out of ten. But that's why we bet."

"Who bets?"

"Everybody bets, especially the women." Koshi was smiling now. "And they cook the loser. Very good."

"Like chicken, huh?"

"Yes, like chicken."

* * * *

I told the base commander someone had alerted me to a snake problem. I was going to arrange a habu management program. I'd need a mongoose master and habu wrangler. I left the hiring to Koshi. The commander told me he was busy with a war and not to bother him about this again.

One week later, we had our first habu fight out behind the club. Since our service clubs already had slot machines, I saw no harm in allowing betting on the outcome of the match.

Our audience sat above and behind a four-foot-high barrier. A mongoose can jump three feet high. The habu isn't a jumper, but big snakes rear up like Cobras. I didn't want any injured fans at my habu fights.

The fights were a hit with our Marine guards and all the Okinawans. Most of the local villagers worked on base as domestics, laborers, or laundresses. Our beer sales doubled and the Awamori whisky sold out on our first fight night. Koshi, always the entrepreneur, arranged barbequing the losers.

The next day, as I went out the main gate, the Marine sentry offered his opinion. "Hey Captain, I tried that habu and it's pretty good. You should try it, sir."

27. November 1951

"Rico, these guys can't make up their minds. Like I told you, two weeks ago, they made me the Assistant Operation Officer for the entire base. Today, I'm out of the job and back flying full time with Bill Williamson in 'B' flight."

"Bitch, bitch, bitch, it gets you back in the air. That's what you wanted, wasn't it?"

I had to agree, flying a plane was more fun than flying a desk. "About that, you are right. You won't be floating from pilot to pilot. You'll be my right seat man, so hopefully this is good news for you too."

"It is, Red. It is."

* * * *

'B' flight was down to five planes. We called our little group "Bill's Boys," and resumed our nightly patrols off the Korean west coast. Major Bill Williamson deployed two F-82s to each patrol sector. Sometimes we were on his wing, sometimes with each of the other crews. Bill kept one plane as a reserve, fueled and ready on the ground. Our few night fighters were the last of the breed until the F-94 jets came into service. Overmatched by jets, we put our advantages of long range and radar to their best possible use.

Navy night fighters based in Japan covered the Korean east coast. Carrier-based jets also patrolled the west coast of Korean sectors. Intruders were few and most of our calls were for ground support interdictions. We'd sweep down from the black of the sky, shoot up enemy truck convoys or troop concentrations, and vanish into the night.

* * * *

"Guys, we've got something special. Night after tomorrow, a sub, the *USS Perch*, is going to drop Royal Commandos for a raid in the North. Their target is to blow up a train inside a railroad tunnel. We will fly top cover and since this is one of our regular patrol zones, our presence shouldn't alert the Reds. Questions?"

"Major, what time will the landing happen?" asked Danny Wiley, radar man in the second plane. He and his pilot, Gene Freitas, sat opposite Rico and me in the briefing room.

"They go ashore at zero dark thirty. The *Perch* has been modified to carry a motor launch. The Navy will have a coxswain and three guys with submachineguns who'll stay with the launch while the Brits go in."

"Your two planes are the cavalry who'll ride to the rescue if this goes bad. You'll get any distress call from squadron command. We still can't link our radios to the Navy. Stupid, huh?" No one among our five crews disagreed with that.

Our five planes waited, gassed and ready for the next night's mission. Four of us took off at half an hour after sundown, two planes for each patrol zone, along the west coast of Korea. Gene and Danny flew off my left wing. Besides full loads of bullets and HVARs, we each carried napalm.

"Here we go, Rico. We should be on station about now. I plan to keep the coast in sight. That way, we may see something before we hear anything from base."

"Good idea, Red. At 2400 I'm switching my radar to ground setting. We may not see the sub. There's no moon tonight, which is probably why the mission is scheduled." We kept to our usual routine flight path and altitude, where the Koreans expected us to be.

"Gabriel flight, this is Naha. Go. Repeat, go."

"Rico, I'm going in. The coast and the rail line will be our landmarks. Gabriel two, did you copy?" When I heard back a "yes" from Gene, I angled slightly right toward land. "I'm dropping to 4,000."

"We got it, Red. We'll stay on your wing." As we descended, muzzle flashes on the ground told their tale. The Brits were retreating toward the coast. Two groups of enemies were pouring in fire and trying to flank our commandos. Small arms fire only so far. What needed to be done was apparent.

"Gabe two, drop to 1,000. You take the left group; I've got the right. We want to stay between the Brits and the hostiles. Let's kick some commie ass. Go!"

"Rico, I've got the napalm. You've got the HVAR bursts, four at a time. I'm going to drop and wheel around right, then come in again and give em' the guns and more HVARS." In the heat of the firefight, I thought the enemy was too busy to scan the skies for me. Our napalm would give them a warm welcome. And in we went.

"Gabe two, drop napalm on my signal, hold-hold-hold; DROP NOW. I felt the bump of the napalm tanks' release at the same moment that four HVARs roared away. The rockets and jellied gasoline hit at the same moment. The ground under us burst into flame. I banked hard right and came around for a strafing run.

I could hear bullets pinging off our plane, up through the fire and smoke below. It looked like the commandos had made it to the beach, but our work was not done.

"Gene, I'll hit em again. You cover the motor launch and the sub. Any patrol boats are all yours. Let me know when the launch reaches the sub, and I'll catch up with you."

Once more, we hit them in a fast pass that arched over both groups in a wide spiral. Their muzzle flashes were fewer now. Our weapons had done their work. I headed back to join my wingman for as long as it took to get our sub safely away.

The sub's black hull lay invisible in the ink-black sea. The only lights were the quick flicks of flashlight beams between the sub and the motor launch. "Rico, vector me to any inbound patrol boats." Luckily none appeared.

We watched as multiple flashlights signaled the Perch's crew was helping the British commandos back aboard. My last view was of the sub vanishing into the inky depths. Suddenly a thermite grenade flared into a dazzling ball of light as the motor launch was abandoned and left to burn. The firelight showed that it was alone on the surface. I checked in with Naha's control and we resumed our normal patrol.

Back on the ground at Naha, Bill Williamson told us they had killed one Brit. But they laid pressure charges under the rail tracks before a patrol discovered them and all hell broke loose. If we blew the tunnel up, I never found out. But I doubted it had. Our enemies were evil but not stupid.

The year ended but no ceasefire was attained, as armistice negotiations dragged on since June 1951.

28. Kojo, April 1952

Sometimes fate hands us a serendipitous opportunity. Sometimes the same finger of fate that beckoned you in changes and just gives you the finger. Rico and I were to take part in a training exercise. We were told just enough to get us to our destination, Napunja, Okinawa. Napunja is on a small peninsula that juts out into the Yellow Sea. An Army regiment was there for amphibious landing training.

By coincidence, the Combined Fleet had gathered in the Sea of Japan. With the Armistice talks dragging on into their twenty-first month, perhaps a show of force might encourage the Reds to settle?

Ninety ships, including four aircraft carriers, arrived off Kojo at the port of Wonsan. The Battleship Iowa, two heavy cruisers, and scores of destroyers started shelling the Kojo coast. Our carrier planes strafed and bombed our landing zone.

They loaded thousands of US Army cavalry troop aboard ships in Japan, a fact immediately known to the Reds. Paratroopers were known to be practicing for an airborne assault. Both our A and B flights from Naha went to Seoul, where we began flying night cover and interdiction patrol over the landing zone. During the day, Navy jets dominated the skies and F-51s strafed anything that moved near the beach. On D-Day thirty plane loads of paratroopers took off before dawn from Japan and simultaneously seven waves of landing craft headed for the beach.

* * * *

"Rico, did you see what I saw?" Here came the thirty transport planes loaded with paratroopers. And then, instead of dropping troops, they turned back. *What the hell?* The Navy had been shelling the landing zone for days. Why turn back?

"Something must have happened, but what?" Rico wondered.

Our radio stayed silent, so any news or explanation wouldn't come until back on the ground in Seoul. With daylight approaching, it was time to head for the base. We headed for the coast and the protection of naval airpower. When the clouds parted, waves of landing craft floated beneath us. The first landing craft sat already at the beach. But no troops? I dropped down for a better view.

"I'm not seeing anybody on the beach. No shooting, no bodies, I mean nobody and nothing. Have I been in the air too long?"

Rico's reply came short seconds later. "Nobody. I see nobody. Red, this is the weirdest thing."

We headed away from the beach to the expected safety of the open sea.

And then it happened.

White balloons of light were rapidly rising from the first destroyer that came into view. We were being shot at! *But we're the good guys.* We were an unexpected visitor, flying toward them in a hot combat zone. The navy gunners saw us as a threat, and they reacted, probably as I would have done in their place.

Bang! The first balloon arrived, striking my fuselage behind the wing. The plane bucked from the anti-aircraft shell strike. I didn't need to tell Rico; our situation was immediate and obvious. As the pilot, the decision was mine. Bail out or crash land?

"Rico, open all radio channels. Tell our HQ that we're taking friendly fire from the Navy and going down. I'm putting her in the drink. We're too low to safely bail out. Our chutes would be no better than umbrellas." Through the smoke rising in my cockpit, he gave me a thumbs up sign.

I dropped us down and slowed my airspeed. The F-82 had a good glide ratio, so we wouldn't fall like a stone. I didn't want to continue toward the ships. Too many Navy gunners remembered the Kamikazes.

"We pop canopies as soon as we're in the water and stopped. Can you tell how bad they hit the plane?" I had to rely on Rico's eyes. I couldn't turn around.

"Your tail assembly and the back of the fuselage are gone. Are you hurt?" Adrenaline kept me focused and unaffected by any pain. "Red, you will not have much control, and you're smoking."

I could hear my heartbeat overlapping with my breathing as I checked myself: hands, arms, torso, legs. I reached behind my back, feeling for wet, warm blood. And there it was, on my left, below my ribs. But still no pain. How bad I couldn't tell, thankfully for the moment.

"I'm good," I lied. But with limited controls, I still had to get us down. The water rolled a hundred feet below, now. How high are the waves? I did not know, but it didn't matter. We'd soon find out.

I kept the landing gear up to smooth the landing and cut the Allisons off. "Hold on. Brace."

The waves were no softer than the tree tops we'd plowed through in Denmark. I kept us from going under, and we came to a stop, still afloat for the moment. The missing tail of my fuselage caused my side to settle almost immediately.

"Canopies off, canopies off" With my seat harness unbuckled, I worked myself to standing and got the first twinge of pain. Our wings had stayed intact and kept us afloat. We had no raft nor flotation devices; we weren't supposed to go down over the water. I climbed out onto the wing. My escape route had taken us about a mile back toward the beach and away from the destroyer.

"Red, nice landing," he said from the boom between our cockpits. "So now we wait for a ride, huh?" A rhetorical question, but the closest to humor he had at the moment.

"Did you raise anybody on the radio?"

"I got through to control and told them our position and situation." All I could do was nod and signal with a thumbs up. I held on to the cockpit rail with one hand. Inside, water covered my seat and was rising fast. If my side went under, I'd be taking Rico's fuselage with me to the bottom of the Sea of Japan.

The waves of silver gray swelled a good six feet before dropping us into their trough. Their unbroken sheet of silk or cellophane oscillated up and down, moved by an unseen engine somewhere beneath. My side throbbed. When I checked for blood, it was there, but that was all I could tell.

Then, above the sounds of the sea, I heard the thumping of helicopter blades. A Navy rescue chopper came into view. A harness descended from the blue helo body.

"Red, you go first. We Italians float real well. I'll be right behind you." I put my arms through the padded canvas of the rescue harness. When I lowered it to my waist, it hurt. I grabbed the harness just below the winch cable. Up I rose fifty feet to the helo door, and they pulled me in. Seeing the blood on my flight suit, a medic directed me to a waiting stretcher. I lay down and everything faded to black.

* * * *

I awoke to the gray metal walls of a sickbay. "Welcome back sir," said the Navy corpsman. My mind was anything but clear as I blinked and struggled to focus through the fog of anesthesia. An IV needle was in my left forearm, and it hurt to breathe.

"Where am I? Where is my partner?"

"This is the USS Antietam, Captain. One of our helos fished you and your radar man out of the drink. Capt. Banducci is fine. I'll let him know you're awake when you are ready for a visitor."

"What happened to me?" My voice probably slurred, but I couldn't tell. It seemed so very hard to focus. My words didn't come by themselves but required a mental assembly to penetrate the fog of anesthesia.

"The doctor will be in soon. Try to relax and your head will clear. You had surgery just hours ago."

My body took the orderly's advice. I closed my eyes and stopped struggling to form thoughts.

Time has a way of standing still when anesthesia blanks your senses and gray windowless walls surround you. The Navy doc explained, the shrapnel had penetrated my abdomen and injured my bowel. Surgery was successful. A month of healing lay ahead. In a few days, I'd go to an Army hospital in Tokyo. After the doctor left, I finally saw Banducci.

"Hey there." And then came the usual series of questions. How did I feel? What happened to me? How long would I be down?

"I wanted to bring you a present, but the gift shop was out of dirty books and cheap booze. Sorry." I knew there was no gift shop, but I was glad for the company. I asked if he'd been wounded. He hadn't.

"What happened to the Kojo landing?" At this, Rico leaned in closer to my sickbed and answered in little more than a whisper. "It was a hoax. They never planned to land. Army Psyops dropped leaflets basically saying, 'We can do this, when and where we want. You assholes need to stop fighting.'" From his facial expression I could tell this was the straight dope.

"The Air Force is pissed. Apparently, the Navy and Army didn't tell them. We lost five planes over Kojo." At this news, I closed my eyes and shook my head in disbelief. "We've been ordered not to talk about Kojo. Capiche?"

I nodded.

"So, what happens now?"

I relayed what the Doc had told me. Then I asked about him.

"The Navy is flying me to Tokyo with you," and he smiled. "Red, I want you to know, while I'm on R & R leave, with every drink I'm having, I'll be thinking of you. All those days and nights alone in Tokyo clubs and bathhouses, you'll be missed. Honest," and he gave me his biggest shit-eating grin.

* * * *

We made it to Tokyo. For the next three weeks, they confined me to bed or a wheelchair as my insides healed. Then a week of being able to walk the hospital grounds using a cane. Rico visited most every day.

Finally, my new orders arrived. I was on a medical hold because of my line of duty injury. When cleared, I'd report to the 3625th Flight Training Squadron at Tyndall AFB in Panama City, Florida. I was to be a fighter pilot instructor.

But first Rico and I returned to Okinawa. I cleared quarters, coordinated travel, and turned over my general duties to a series of successors. "Banducci, be sure to look me up when you get to Florida."

"Red, it's been a pleasure flying with you. And you look me up if you're ever in McAlester, Oklahoma."

* * * *

It helped that I had managed the club, been nice to everybody and never acted like an asshole. The base commander was happy to convert my Medical Hold status to a Convalescent Temporary Duty at Tripler Hospital, Hickam Field, Hawaii. He required that I have my 'fit for duty' status checked every thirty days and reported back to him. No problem.

I was on the next transport plane headed for Hawaii. Our route was the reverse of the path we'd taken from Hawaii to Okinawa. My ride was in a C-119 cargo plane, which we called the "flying boxcar." The C-119 had twin booms like the old P-38, but between the booms was its fat cylindrical body. The entire rear of the plane could open hydraulically.

We usually used the boxcars to carry parachute troops. In the spring of 1950, the C-119s had kept the Army and Marines fighting at the Chosin reservoir supplied with beans and bullets. When the Marines made their fighting retreat under relentless attack by the Chinese, the boxcars saved them by dropping bridging equipment to replace a destroyed bridge that blocked their retreat.

Our seats were canvas, one piece like a hammock, but divided into seat and back by a rod behind my butt. The rod kissed my tailbone with every bump. No windows in the cargo bay of the C-119. The twin rotary engines propelled us low and slowly through the tropic skies. And they were loud. It was a toss-up with leaving Sweden in the converted bomb bay of a B-24 for the worst ride of my life.

The cargo area was wide enough to accommodate a jeep, so there was room to stand, move about, or lie flat out on the aluminum deck. My rank and status as a combat pilot made me welcome to come up to the flight deck. Three steps above the cargo bay, the flight deck accommodated the four-man crew. I was welcome to stand between their seats and admire the view. "Water, water everywhere."

Our mid-flight meal came in a brown cardboard box. The cheese sandwich on white bread, banana and cookies were washed down with either water or coffee. The same gourmet's delight every day. But I should quit bitching, because I was on my way to Hawaii. Okinawa to Kwajalein, then to Midway and finally on to the island of my dreams.

* * * *

Arriving on Oahu, I checked in at Tripler Medical Center. I was told to report back in a month's time. Their medical holding company and Visiting Officers' Quarters were both full of other returnees from Korea, so I was going to the Royal Hawaiian Hotel. Life was getting better. With 400 rooms in its six stories and the exterior all painted pink, it fronted 15 acres of private beach.

As soon as I felt it was safe, I resumed my routine of running and stretching. Flying planes required strength and endurance, but not as much as evading capture did.

I took a cab to the Navy base, showed my military ID, and walked out to survey what had been Battleship Row at Ford Island. Seven of our nine battleships had been there on December 7, 1941. Oily black tears rose from the wreck of the

USS Arizona. The sheen of gold, pink, green and blue marked the watery grave of her 1,177 crewmen entombed below.

The Filipino barmen at the Royal Hawaiian were attentive to all their customers, most especially those in the US military. Mauricio was the day shift barman; Cristanto and Luis were on the night shift in the Terrace Bar. I soon learned their version of English, which was every bit as understandable as the southernese of Dusty Rhodes.

"Captain Black, you Americans saved the Pillowpeno people. I got your drinks covered sir. Puck the Japs. You and the pair of pliers at the end of the bar are my guests."

I looked up and acknowledged the two Navy guys in their dress whites sitting at the end of the bar. In the background, the music of Harry Owens and his Royal Hawaiians filled the orchid-scented air. The two took their drinks to a nearby table and gestured for me to join them. And I did.

Even before anyone spoke, their emblems of rank told me they were Lieutenants, my equivalent rank. The gold wings and shield superimposed over an anchor meant they were also pilots. They greeted me with outstretched hands.

"Red Black."

"Ken Pilaeri," said the taller of the two. "And this is my wingman, Bill Matroni. Have a seat, Captain." Handshakes now exchanged, we recognized each other as fellow fliers. "We're from carrier air group 11, on the *Kearsarge*," said Pilaeri. "And you?" I knew the *USS Kearsarge* to be an Essex class carrier stationed off the east coast of Korea.

I told them about flying the Twin Mustang for air interdiction patrols and giving top cover to downed flyers. This brought side-long glances between the two. They both responded simultaneously.

"You folks saved a lot of our guys who got shot down. Many thanks," and they both raised their glasses in a salute. I motioned to Luis at the bar for another round of drinks.

"So, what brings you to Hawaii, Red?" inquired Matroni with a smile. "R and R like us?"

"Well, not exactly. I'm on Convalescent TDY to Tripler. We got shot down during the Kojo operation. I took some to the abdomen." As the drinks arrived, I could see their mood change. *Eyes that had been on me were now looking at the tabletop or their buddy.* Neither man spoke, so I continue my story.

"A Navy helo pulled me and my copilot out of the water. I had surgery on the Antietam. A few days later, the Navy flew us to Tokyo." *I needed to change the mood at our table.* "So anyway, thanks right back to the Navy. Your guys pulled us out of the water and a Navy doc patched me up." My attempt to return a compliment hadn't lifted the pall that hung over our table.

Finally, Pileri broke the heavy silence. "Yah, you guys got screwed in the Kojo operation," and he looked across to his mate. "Off the record, we're instructed not to talk about Kojo." Again, only the sound of ice cubes rattling in our glasses was heard. *Message received, the Air Force got screwed by Army and Navy brass. My table mates, like Rico and myself, just followed orders, doing what needed to be done, even at the risk of our lives.*

I changed the subject, hoping to rekindle the camaraderie that had brought us together at the terrace table. "When the doc at Tripler finds me fit for duty, I'm headed to Tyndall in Panama City to teach what I learned over here." It worked and our conversations resumed, now with a safe topic.

"We know Panama City. Bill and I trained at Pensacola. Have you been to Tyndall before, Red?"

I gave a quick "No."

"Pensacola and Panama City are both on the Gulf coast, but you're about 100 miles East of the Naval Air Station. Here's the deal; the beaches are white sand, and the women are friendly to the military, especially fliers. The land is flat. Lots of tree farms, growing lodge pole pines for the paper mills. You'll smell the mills before you see them."

"And it's hot," Bill chimed in. "Oh, and the love bugs swarm for a month in the spring and again in the fall."

Ken nodded in agreement. Perhaps the tilt of my head was enough to convey my ignorance about love bugs, so he pressed on. "Small flying beetles. They swarm by the millions. Here's a tip. Do you have a car waiting for you back in the states?"

"Yes, a Buick convertible. Why?"

"Ok, when the first swarms appear, drive with the top up and the windows closed. If you go through a swarm, your windshield will be speckled black with their bodies. Whatever you do, don't turn on your wipers. That only smears them, and you won't be able to see at all. Trust me."

"So, what should I do?"

Two smiling faces gave the same advice simultaneously. "Go on leave or TDY somewhere."

"And don't breathe through your mouth," added Ken.

* * * *

We set an evening cocktail hour date. Five o'clock at the Terrance Bar, and then we went our separate ways, or sometimes to share dinner or a night in town. I'd made two new friends.

In the days to come, I walked around Honolulu seeing the sights while I could. Flying is a dangerous business, even when no one is shooting at you. At month's end, I got cleared for duty. They relayed this news back to my squadron commander on Okinawa.

The travel gods were smiling when I arranged my trip back to the States. I had the choice of flying to California in an Air Force transport with canvas seats or going by ship.

I made the trip on a Navy transport headed to the Mare Island repair docks at Vallejo. My cabin was simple but clean. I took my meals with the ship's officers. As our arrival time firmed up, the radioman was happy to relay a message to my sister Melba, the babysitter of my Buick, to meet me at the dock. I had ten days from landing in Vallejo to report in at Tyndall AFB.

29. Florida, September 1952

First, I dropped in on my folks in Stockton, then a short overnight visit with my sister, Doris, her husband Phil Scott, and their son, Stuart. This left me eight days to make the 2,500-mile drive to the East Coast. I knew my route: I-40 east from Los Angeles, across Arizona, New Mexico and Texas, then dropping down to the Louisiana Gulf Coast and skirting through Mississippi and into Florida. My orders and ID got me cheap meals and free lodgings at military bases almost every day. The early September weather was hot, so I timed my driving for early starts and early check-ins at my next base. My V-8 Buick Roadmaster roared along, top down mostly. I didn't mind the ten miles per gallon that it got, even at 27 cents a gallon for gas.

My last travel day was from Keesler AFB in Biloxi, Mississippi, to Panama City. Recalling Ken and Bill's warning about Love bugs, I asked about the little bastards before leaving the base.

"Yup, they are swarming in Florida."

Forewarned, I made the last 240 miles with top up and windows closed. I knew I'd have a full day's work cleaning their black bodies off the windows, massive chrome grille, hood and fenders. I made an early start on the five-hour trip, so I would have time to get oriented and settled at my new post.

* * * *

F-86D Sabre Jet Fighter

The Main Gate guards at Tyndall AFB directed me to the 3625th Training Squadron Office. The roar of jets above was a constant background, as I expected at an Air Training Command Base. Driving across the flat landscape, I saw cement runways longer and wider than any I'd seen before. Rows of F-86D all-weather Sabre jets sat across from F-94 Starfire jets. This was the first time I'd seen the F-94 we needed to replace our aging, dwindling supply of Twin Mustangs and Black Widow night fighters.

I was in uniform, captain's silver bars on my collar and a blue plastic name tag pinned above my left breast pocket. My arrival was expected.

"This way, sir," and the clerk escorted me down the hall to the squadron commander's office. He knocked on the door frame, and Lieutenant Colonel Harry Moulton looked up from the papers he'd been reviewing.

"Captain Black, welcome to the 3625th." He stood and offered his hand for me to shake. "Please come in and take a seat." Lt. Col. Moulton had my 201 Personnel file and training records already on his desktop, so he'd reviewed my service record and flight qualifications.

"Captain, you are needed here as much as the F-86Ds are needed over Korea. I'm sure you have heard that our F-80s and F-84s are no match for the MiG 15s. The F-86D, we hope, will even the odds. But our pilots have to be as good as our planes. Your combat experience needs to be communicated to those guys we are sending over to battle the Reds. So far, you've flown our best prop planes, F-51, B-26 and F-82s. Their time has passed. So, first we'll get you certified on the 86s and then put you to work as an instructor. Fair enough?"

"Yes, sir."

"Take today to get settled with Q and finance. Sgt. West will get you oriented and arrange transportation if you need it."

"I have my personal vehicle outside. A map and some simple directions will do just fine, sir."

"Be back here at 0800 tomorrow and I'll introduce you to your trainer."

I gave the expected "Yes, sir," saluted and turned back to the sergeant who'd been waiting outside the commander's door.

Back at the front desk, Sgt. West pulled a map of the base out of his top drawer. "Here's where we are, Captain, and here — I'll circle the spots — are housing, finance, the closest dining facility, O Club, Base Exchange and Class Six store. Can I mark anything else for you, sir?"

"Nope. Q, pay, food and drink. That covers it. Thanks."

By the end of the day, I'd made all the essential stops. Officers' Quarters were on-post in a white cinder block building, surrounded by lawns. The grass was unlike anything I'd ever seen. It snaked horizontally into a low, thick thatch.

My Q was designed for two officers, each with his own room, a shared bath, a combination living room and along one wall what passed for a kitchen. One bedroom was already occupied, so I hung up my uniforms and emptied my satchel into the other bedroom's closet and dresser. I introduced myself to the other occupant, Lieutenant Ed White. He was also at Tyndall for F-86 instructor training.

Introductions made, it was time to eat, organize my finances, find a place to wash the bugs off the Buick and by then, probably cocktail time!

I soon found that Ed White was an agreeable housemate, a friend who understood the dreams that haunted me. Ed had his own collection of unpleasant memories from Korea. After a month of testing our compatibility as housemates, Ed and I decided to share an offpost rental. Where? The Beach was an easy option. Our condo choice was cemented by its location within walking distance of Tony's Beach Cabana Bar and The Silver Slipper restaurant.

* * * *

"Good morning, Colonel," I said as I saluted. I was invited to sit beside a major, already seated opposite Moulton. We were both wearing our olive-gray flight suits, a pilot's usual uniform.

"Captain Black, meet Major Rodgers. He is our senior flight instructor, who trains our F-86D trainers."

Upon being introduced, the major turned my way, smiled, and nodded in greeting.

"Good luck, Captain," said Lt. Col. Mouton, half a beat before adding "Dismissed"

Rodgers and I rose and exited the office. We were only steps out the door when he turned and, with a side-long glance, spoke as we walked.

"Call me Del. Why don't we find coffee and I'll tell you about our schedule. Fair enough?" I nodded in agreement. There was a day room at the opposite end of the hallway, and I could smell coffee as we entered and sat. I noticed Rodgers carried a USAF manual under his arm.

"Captain Black, do you prefer William or Bill?" He poured coffee into paper cups as we talked.

"Actually, I prefer Red."

"Okay, Red, it is. Here's the plan. I've seen your file; you've got a lot of hours in a good number of planes. You've flown the best of their day: the F-51, the B-26 and the F-82 Twin. I flew P-51s in Europe, but I'm here to tell you, if you liked the power of the Mustang, you're going to love the Sabre jet. This morning we'll go out to the field and do a walk around." He slid the manual across our tabletop.

"This is the technical manual on the F-86D. Your homework is to read and reread that puppy until you've committed all the details to memory. Here are some of the chief points to focus on." I leaned back, took a sip of coffee, and gave him my full attention.

"The F-86D is built around a new weapons system, the 70mm 'Mighty Mouse' retractable under-fuselage tray carrying rockets. She has our first afterburner, that will boost your thrust by over 5,400 foot-pounds. It really kicks her in the ass and puts you flat in your seat. This is our new front-line fighter and will be so until the much-troubled F-89 Scorpion comes online in 1954."

"Tomorrow, I'll quiz you on the contents of the manual. This is a single seater, so when we go up, you'll be on my wing. If you screw up, I'll do my best to talk you through the problems, but ultimately you are alone and all I can do is watch you auger in." He added with a half-smile, "So please don't screw up. I hate those 'After Action' reports. Ready?"

I nodded, and we headed for his jeep.

* * * *

My plane was the last in a row of 12 that lined the wide combined taxiway and runways. The concrete river before me stretched for 13,000 feet into the distance and four separate runways ran down its almost half-mile width.

We both had our standard issue dark glasses on already. The glare off the bright aluminum skin of the fighter was more than unshaded eyes could comfortably tolerate. Its nose was painted black above the jet engine intake. They painted the tail red with a large, white capital "T" on it. I took the 'T' to be my 'student driver' fair warning notice to other pilots.

As we circled the plane, Del Rodgers ran a commentary on what we were seeing. He ducked under the fuselage to point out the retractable 'Mighty Mouse' rocket tray. Inside were 24 finned rockets that I could fire in any number I chose. "The aerial fins fold out when the rocket launches and add stability and accuracy to the weapon's path." I had no machine guns to use.

The access ladder already leaned on the left side of the cockpit.

"Have a look and take your seat," said my trainer as he gestured toward the ladder. What I found was mostly nothing new. Del climbed up the ladder behind me and pointed out features that I'd not seen in propeller planes. Chief among the changes were the afterburner switch and the Mighty Mouse fire control system. The new and more sophisticate onboard electronics, while wonderful, would take some getting used to. But that was why I had a manual to study and a personal flight trainer.

Our last stop before lunch was at our squadron's maintenance hangar, where I met MSgt. Andy Anderson, our squadron crew chief. "Master Sergeant, this is my new student, Capt. Red Black."

Anderson saluted us both and after returning his salute, we shook hands.

"That's a very colorful name, Sir."

"Thanks, I guess. It goes with the red hair."

"What time do you want us to have your planes ready, Major?"

"Zero nine hundred, Master Sergeant. Red and I have a quiz to get through first thing tomorrow."

"No worries, Sirs. They'll be ready" We saluted and walked back to the Jeep.

"Red, the afternoon is yours. I suggest you dig into the manual. I need to know that you're up to speed on the plane before we get into the air."

I'd walked from my Q, so he dropped me off at the squadron HQ. Manual in hand, I walked to chow and then on to read and learn what new information I carried in my hand.

* * * *

The next morning, back at the squadron HQ, Maj. Rodgers was waiting.

"All right, did you read the manual?" asked Del. "And you understood what you read, before we go up above Tyndall?"

"I did."

With that, Del Rodgers launch into his quiz about the F-86 technical manual. His questions were straightforward, direct, and pointed. Either I knew this stuff or I didn't. He asked, and I answered.

"What's the stall speed?"

"124."

"How do you handle a mid-air engine shutdown?"

"Throttle down, point the nose down and slowly raise your throttle setting back up."

"Maximum range and fuel consumption rates?"

"Thirty gallons per minute, except with afterburner, which takes you to 80 gallons per minute. With drop tanks adding 200 gallons per tank and a maximum of 4 tanks, max range is 835 miles."

"Maximum speed and elevation?"

"715 mph and 49,000 feet."

His questions covered all the essential points in the manual. But you only knew that when you had enough experience and awareness to acknowledge "what you didn't know." The quiz continued. Ejection seat operation, gross weight, and propulsion. I had to grasp the contents of the manual to assure Del I wouldn't kill myself on my initial flight.

"Red, you passed my abbreviated ground school. Now that you've memorized all the information about the D, I'll tell you, we should get the F series soon. The F has a better GE engine, better wing flight controls and six Browning machine guns. Also, their gunsight is radar linked to automatically compensate for distance. Underwing rockets are optional, depending on the mission." He paused and smiled.

"As you probably have figured out in your ten years, the Air Force doesn't learn fast, but they learn good."

I acknowledged this truth about our bosses with a smile.

"One last thing. We now have G-suits. They keep the blood from pooling in your legs and minimize the chance of you having a 'gray out.' It's your choice if you want one or not. I suggest, after our flight today, you consider trying one.

"Let's get you in the air. What do you think?"

"Yes, let's go for it." We headed out to the flight line. As arranged yesterday, both our planes were ready to go. I climbed the five steps up the ladder, dropped into the cramped cockpit and signaled I'd follow my trainer's lead.

* * * *

The ground crew started our engines with their external power units, removed our ladders and withdrew to a safe distance. I nudged my throttle forward to follow my trainer out onto the taxiway.

The front wheel assembly seemed weak, undersized perhaps, and wobbled as we taxied. I stopped behind Maj. Rodgers on the runway and watched as they cleared him to take off. Then it was my turn.

"Tower, this is T-1."

"Go, T-1. The runway is yours." I pulled the stick towards my lap and began to move forward. The plane was slow to respond, so I pulled more. Then its gentle roll changed, and I was leaping into the air. This bird was different from all my rides on prop planes. When the General Electric jet engine hit its sweet spot, up we rose. I made a mental note to find the 'tells' so I could expect the jump from rolling to rising. I especially wanted to know; can I power up faster? Shorten the roll and quicken the jet jump from ground to air?

Aloft now, I raised the landing gear and established radio contact with my trainer. "T-1 to T, I have you visually. I'm coming to your wing."

"That's a roger, T-1. Tuck in behind my right wing and we'll begin your lessons."

"Roger that, T, coming now." The sky was bright and clear. My canopy was like the F-82's, clear plexiglass, with a minimum of frame components fixed and forward facing. Del allowed us to fly straight and level for a good 10 minutes. "Just get the feel of your plane, for now."

"T-1, ready on my mark; we're going to afterburners." He led, and I followed. And what a jolt it was. The engine roared instantaneously with a 50 percent increase in power. My airspeed rose rapidly from 350 mph to over 650. My torso got pushed back into the molded seat frame. The unseen forces of nature changed my tight lips into a grimace. My lower body experienced a downward pushing. *What the hell? What invisible force is sitting on my lap, squeezing my torso and forcing the blood to my legs?*

"Red, are you still with me? Cut your afterburner. That's enough for now. Come back to your wing spot and signal when ready for lesson numero dos."

Finding my voice as the pressure relaxed, I responded, "Si, mi Capitan."

"Ok, now we're going up to our max altitude. At 49,000 she is starving out. For today, don't push it. Level off and enjoy the view. You'll being seeing the curvature of the earth from a new vantage point. Understood?"

"Roger, T," and up we climbed at 12,000 feet per minute. As Del had warned me, the atmosphere and my engine didn't get along. It now felt like I was dragging a lead sled. My thighs seemed to swell, and the first tinges of light-headedness came upon me. High above drifting banks of clouds, the curvature of the earth showed in the distance.

"Red, we're going to descend and head back to the barn. Tomorrow we'll repeat today's moves and add a new maneuver or two. Let's get together at squadron ops and go over today's flight. Roger that?"

"Heard," and we began our descent. As I flew along, tucked behind the major's wing, the aeronautical perfection of this bird was clear. The swept-back wing and its purity of line made the F-86 a dream to fly. I was looking forward to getting back in the air tomorrow.

The glide ratio of her design made landing easy, and I touched down with my power throttled back. Back on the ground, the front landing gear wheel still annoyed me. But if this was my only quibble after a day in the air, I'd cope.

Master Sgt. Anderson's ground crew was ready and waiting as we taxied off the runway and up the adjoining taxiway to our hard stands. With our engines off, the access ladders appeared as our cockpit canopies opened. We'd been in the air for the better part of two hours. I stood up in the cockpit and flexed my knees as my circulation returned to normal. Sure that I could negotiate the ladder now, I climbed down to the tarmac. Del Rodgers met me and together we climbed into the Master Sgt's. jeep and rode back to the squadron HQ.

"What do you think, Red?"

"I think that tomorrow, I'm going to wear a G-suit."

* * * *

We were back at it the next morning and every morning for the next two weeks. A G-suit was now standard to my daily attire. Like a tight-fitting pair of pants, it kept the blood from leaving my upper body, pooling in my legs and bringing a deadly gray to my mind.

Each day, we repeated previous lessons. Finally, muscle memory made critical maneuvers automatic. We added aerial restart procedures, so much a life-or-death skill to perfect in case the engines quit on me. Hearing Del telling me to starve out the jet engine was shocking, nonetheless.

"Point her nose down toward the ground, wait 10 seconds, and slowly throttle back up." This seemed so wrong, in so many ways, but I did it. *Well, if this all turns to shit, at least I am in a functional glider. I probably won't auger in.* Somewhere between having learned to follow orders and trusting my plane, I did as told.

"Roger that. Oh, and if this works, the first drink at the O Club is on me tonight. Here goes nothing." And it worked!

* * * *

As the days went on, my trust in the plane grew. We added maneuvers to test the F-86's agility. Hard rolls left or right, corkscrew maneuvers or rapid ascents or descents all came easily to this aircraft. As my confidence grew, I tried out every maneuver I could think of. And the plane never failed me. I knew from F-86 pilots in Korea that the MiG 15s out-climbed and out-maneuvered us. So, I had to train better pilots than our opponents, until we had our own plane that outmatched the MiG.

I was essentially flying on my own now as Del turned me loose from behind his wing. His observing and tutoring now came from a distance. One evening over a drink in the O Club, Maj. Rodgers previewed the next phase of my training.

"Tomorrow we'll fly out to the firing range and get you oriented to the Mighty Mouse system. The rockets are finned, so more accurate than the HVARs we've been using."

I nodded, signifying I understood, but resisted speaking my mind. *I'd feel a hell of a lot better if I had guns, too.* But Del said it for me.

"I liked the Browning .50 cals that we had in the Mustangs. I understand the F-86Fs that should be out in the next ninety days have six of them. But we got what we got, for now." We clicked glasses, my Martell's and soda against his beer.

"I guess tomorrow I'll find out if they are Mighty Mouse or Mickey Mouse."

* * * *

For the next two days, under Del's supervision, I practiced firing the rockets at ground targets. There was little difference from the HVARs that I'd been using. I controlled the number from the 24 rockets on board that I loosed at any one time. Unlike in the Twin Mustang, firing large numbers of rockets in a single salvo didn't make this plane buck.

On our third day, I was hunting airborne targets hauled behind T-33 tow planes. Now I understood the advantage of having fins on the 2.75-inch diameter rockets.

My onboard electronics helped me sight my barrage to the target aircraft. At Del's suggestion, I'd fire in four rocket bursts, then check for results before firing any more. The rockets were plane killers, if I hit my target.

After three weeks of tutelage, Del gave me the next week on my own, to fly as much as possible, practicing my skills. He entered into my training record that I was now qualified on the F-86D. What the 3625th Training Squadron had in mind for me was as yet unknown. But at least I was qualified as an F-86 interceptor instructor.

At the end of my month of training, Lt. Col. Moulton asked for me to report to his office. I expected to meet other instructors. It didn't happen.

"Capt. Black, Maj. Rodgers has signed off on your training. Both your attitude and how well you mastered the F-86D impressed him. Congratulations, that's high praise indeed." It gratified me to hear the positive comments from Del.

"He's recommended you for the advanced course that's being taught up at Moody AFB. I'm sending you TDY. Your class begins in two weeks, on October 10th. I'm adding five days for travel and to get you situated on the base. Questions for me?"

"No, sir." I had questions, but I'd track down Del Rodgers and ask him. And with that, I was dismissed.

I found Maj. Rodgers in the squadron operations center, where my questions were asked and answered. "Red, as the war drags on, the supply of experienced fighter pilots is not enough. We want the next generation of fighter pilots to learn from combat veterans what is necessary to stay alive." Then he paused, his fingers drumming on the tabletop.

"Honestly, the MiG is still a better plane than anything we're flying. So, it's our job to produce better pilots. At Moody, you're going to learn the tricks of the trade from guys who've flown against the MiGs. I want you to bring those skills and tricks back here to Tyndall and hammer them into your students. If you can do that, you'll be saving lives."

30. Moody AFB, Valdosta, GA

I'd never been to Moody AFB or even to the state of Georgia. As I made the three-hour drive north through Tallahassee and into Georgia, the humidity lessened. I'd never minded heat since Stockton and the Central Valley. As I joked with friends, "Hell doesn't worry me, because it's a dry heat." Anyway, the land was the same ubiquitous flat ground, covered in palmetto and piss pole pine plantations, as most of the Gulf Coast.

The love bug season was done; I wouldn't have to deep clean the Buick upon arrival. Orders presented, quarters assigned, and directions given to our schoolhouse, the Advanced Interceptor class.

As expected, they had given me a two-man room, configured the same as my quarters at Tyndall: separate bedrooms with a shared bath and living room/kitchen. The Air Force was not concerned with style, so the buildings were the same as on any other base. I was first to arrive in the room. My uniforms and civilian attire hung up, I headed out to find the essentials: the O Club and how to get to Atlanta. After announcing my arrival to the school, I planned to play tourist.

Getting ready for my trip had taken one day, the drive to Valdosta another. With a one-day margin of safety, I had two days left over, and Atlanta was only three hours north. I loaded up the Buick with my valise and put my sport coat, slacks, dress shirts and ties back in a garment bag. In my wallet, a surplus $1,000 fun money.

After Europe, I'd traded baseball for poker as my favorite form of relaxation. Like many of the pilots I served with, gambling for money came easy after a day of gambling with our lives.

Straight poker was a gentlemen's game, so proper dress and manners were essential. I checked into the old Candler Hotel near the center of town. My sister Doris would call it a 'Grand Hotel.' I just called it expensive, but it had the right atmosphere.

A valet parked my Buick in their underground garage. I passed over five dollars and asked that the Buick get washed.

I found the bar, ordered a drink, *it's five o'clock somewhere*, tipped ten dollars and asked if there was a gentleman's card game anywhere round. I showed my military ID to put aside any fears that I was some kind of criminal agent. If anyone knew where to find a game, it would be a high-end bartender. Thus reassured and impressed by the tip, the man behind the bar suggested I come back at nine PM. When I returned, he passed over a room number and a poker chip, nothing more. I left another ten on the bar with my sincere thanks.

At room 505, a white-coated waiter answered the door. "Sir, this is a private party. Do you have an invitation?"

I passed over the single chip.

"Please come in, sir. May I take your jacket, sir?"

"No, thank you," I replied.

Before me was a large round table with eight chairs and seven guests. Not until they laid the hand down did any of the seven look my way. Neither green eye shades nor arm garters showed. The seven men were all in shirts and ties. Some smoked, some drank, but all eyed me as I claimed my seat and removed ten one-hundred-dollar bills from my billfold.

Now two porters descended on me, and one took my drink order, "tonic water with a twist." The other porter rolled up a service cart carrying trays of brightly colored chips. This was the bank. First, I was told the rules for the table: straight poker. Twenty-dollar buy-in per hand. Now I chose my chips accordingly: twenties, fifties and hundreds. Then the deck passed to me for the next deal.

As I shuffled, I spoke. "Gentlemen, thank for allowing me a seat at your table. I will end my evening at the stroke of two AM, win or lose, unless I'm financially insolvent before then. I mention that only in the unlikely event that I am ahead at two AM." I passed the shuffled deck to the player on my right. "Cut," and the game began.

As cards will do, my luck ebbed and flowed, but at two AM I was $1200 ahead. Two other players joined my exit, but not before I received an invitation to return the following night. I took my winnings and left.

The next day, I was up late. The "Do not Disturb" sign kept intruders away. After my toilet and a late breakfast — no, make that brunch — I headed out to see something of Atlanta. First stop, the Coca-Cola Museum, some five blocks away. I puzzled over how so many streets shared the name "Peach Tree," but I saw no peaches. I never did find out why.

After Coca-Cola, I walked to the Georgia Aquarium. I'd never been in an aquarium before and happily spent two hours looking at the fish as they looked back at me. At four PM I returned to the hotel for my one cocktail of the day, an excellent dinner and a nap. The game resumed at nine PM, and I planned to be back in my seat. At the mahogany bar for my only Martell's and soda of the day, I thanked my benefactor behind the bar and left a twenty under my empty glass.

Back at 505, the faces of porters and players were now familiar, and I took my seat. With another $1,000 changed to chips, we began. Tonight, there was some small amount of conversation between players. The bankers, merchants, lawyers, and doctors acknowledged my service around the table. Once again, at my first deal, I announced my departure time, "unless you've lightened my load prior to that time." They didn't, and I departed at two AM, another $1,500 to the good for tonight.

* * * *

Back at Moody AFB, with a day to spare. The Advanced Interceptor flight school began the following Monday. As expected, I found my classmates to all be experienced fighter pilots. These were instructors like me, flight or squadron leaders, the keepers of our fighter pilot culture. I renewed acquaintances with long-time friends and got updates on their present postings. My friend, Greg Gagnon, was also an F-86 pilot trainer. His duty station was out at Nellis AFB, just north of Henderson, Nevada.

The class was small — ten attendees — so while we waited for our instructor to arrive, I introduced myself to those whom I hadn't met. "Red Black," and offered my one free hand.

"Carl Cashdollar. Pleased to meet you, Red."

"What do you do for Uncle Sam?" I asked and sipped my cup of coffee.

"I just took over as operations officer for the 21st Fighter Wing. They've attached us to the SAC. I fly out of Ramstein, Germany. I've spent my career protecting our bombers. I flew P-51 cover for our 8th Air Force guys out of Norwich."

"No kidding. I was a B-24 navigator out of Hethel. You guys were our sheepdogs. I owe you a drink at the O club."

As Carl smiled in acknowledgment, I heard someone enter behind us. It was our instructor, and I knew of him: Major John Bolt, the first F-86 Ace. John had been with the 51st Fighter Group, where I'd served for a while on Okinawa.

"Gentlemen, if you'd take your seats, I'll keep the bullshit to a minimum and get us up in the air. This class will be long on practice, based on what I've seen in Korea, flying the F-86 A and B. I'll tell you what worked and how we exploited the few places where our new F-86Ds are superior to the MiG 15s. I learned what their planes could do and what their pilots would probably do. Up to now, Russian or Chinese pilots flew the MiGs, and those guys were good. They learned their stuff fighting Germans and Japs, just like we did.

"The MiG could climb higher than I could. So, I went high before he did. Because I had a better dive speed, the advantage switched to me. I was more maneuverable, so I could cut inside or away from the MiG and he couldn't follow. That's how I killed them before they could kill me.

"Now, here is where we are today. Our D variant has the same maximum altitude as the MiG, and we can still out-turn and out-dive them. Our Ds are faster than the enemy and soon we'll have the Brownings, and not those Mickey Mouse rockets. Finally, we will be in a better bird. So, until the enemy comes out with their next generation fighter, we can own the air.

"We will fly F-86D variants, and we'll have a chalk-talk out on the tarmac every morning at 0800. On the ground, I will explain a maneuver. Then I'll be up in the air with you. We'll rendezvous at a pre-set altitude and vector, then I'll demonstrate the move. After the demonstration, you'll each attempt the maneuver under my supervision. This is a pass, no-fail situation. You show me and you pass. You keep showing me until you pass."

For the next two weeks, we watched, learned, and practiced the lessons from our only F-86 Ace. Bolt gave us call signs that included a number, one through 10. As I got to know my nine classmates, those instructors and squadron leaders, I knew we would train better pilots than our foe.

* * * *

At the end of our duty day, most of our class ended up sharing either drinks, dinner, or both. Half our group was going back to assignments supporting the SAC. The F-86 was the Cold War replacement for the P-51, protecting their bombers, even though its operational range was more limited than the F-82.

My poker partner, Greg Gagnon, was going back to Nellis AFB to train pilots. Next at the poker table, Glen Lanier would return to his fighter squadron in Japan. Irv Posner, poor bastard, was going to Eielson AFB in Fairbanks, Alaska. The fourth at our table was Carl Cashdollar, the former P-51 pilot, now flying out of Ramstein, Germany. As Gagnon shuffled the cards, I launched into a story.

"In July of '45 we hit a marshalling yard in Munich, dropping 2,000-pound ordnance. The 2,000-pounders are 14 feet long and have two shackles holding them in our bomb bay. Anyway, one shackle failed to open, and we had five feet of armed bomb dangling below our bomb bay doors, which we couldn't close. We were inside the German anti-aircraft box over Munich and if the bomb got hit with on our way out, it would explode. So, we circled inside the box while we tried to free the bomb.

"One P-51 from our escort group stayed with us over Munich while we worked on the shackle. That pilot deserved a medal." Gagnon's shuffling was over, and our table was silent as I finished the story.

"So, that was you? Well, I'll be damned," said Carl Cashdollar. "I'm glad you made it back, Red."

All eyes were upon us, as I stood up from the table and saluted Carl. "Carl, you are one of the reasons that I stayed in and became a fighter pilot." I was at a table full of heroes. "Greg, deal the cards."

* * * *

What I learned at Moody, I drilled into my students at Tyndall. These hard-won lessons, and our next generation F-86Fs, which arrived in January 1953, gave us mastery of the air until the mid-1950's when the MiG 17 debuted.

F-86F Sabre Jet Fighter

31. Returning to Normal, 1960

As a support element for the worldwide SAC mission, my duties began taking me on regular trips to SAC headquarters at Offutt AFB in Omaha, Nebraska. I noticed something about myself in my 30s. I wasn't looking at secretaries or women as dating material. I was now looking at them and evaluating their long-term possibilities. Could I envision her as a wife and mother? Was this someone who, without make-up and a hairdo, I'd want to wake up next to for the next 50 or more years?

The first woman that caught my eye was Shelley Candler. Behind her desk at Offutt and deeper behind the propriety of a high-necked dress that the times and the job required, there was something else. But what exactly? I tried to find out.

"Ms. Candler, I'm..."

She stopped me mid-sentence. "I know who you are, Major Black. What can I do for you?"

A smile accompanied the answer, so onward I pushed. "I'm TDY. I'd like a companion for dinner. Would you do me the honor?"

"Why Major, are you asking me out? On a date?" Still smiling back at me, Shelley was interested, maybe intrigued, and anything but uncomfortable with my offer. *I'm obviously not the first pilot who's asked her out.*

"Yes Major, I'd be happy to be your dinner guest. Would you like me to suggest a restaurant, since you are from out of town?"

I also agreed to having her make the dinner reservation. I left with her off-post address in hand and enough time to wash the Buick after my duty day ended.

"Well, hello. You are right on time," she said. Her evening frock, chiffon printed with pink summer flowers, left her shoulders bare. On her tanned skin, I could see part of an intricate snake tattoo. The scaled body came over her left shoulder and descended below the bodice of the dress to parts unknown. *Lucky snake.*

"Did you expect anything less?"

This brought a smile to her lips, and that's when I noticed the small blonde girl peering around her mother's thigh at the tall stranger at the door.

I squatted down to eye level with the child. "Well, hello there, I'm Bill. Are you my other dinner guest?" She answered with a negative shake of her head and Shelley's hand eased the child out from hiding.

"This is Daphne. Daphne is in for the night, I'm afraid. She has a date with the bathtub and bed." And with that, Shelley bent to kiss her daughter good night, then turned and directed the girl into the care of an older woman who waited several feet away.

"Shall we go?"

I stepped back and walked at Shelley's side to my new 1960 Buick Electra convertible.

"This is beautiful, Major," she said, running one hand over the champagne gold metallic finish.

"Top up or top down?" I asked solicitously as I opened the passenger side door.

"Ooh, how about top down? If you don't mind my hair getting a little mussed?"

I didn't mind. I hope to mess it myself sometime. "So, top down it is, yes ma'am." Now seated beside her, I started the engine and pressed the dashboard button. We watched the top retract to the space behind the saddle-leather back seats.

"Where are you taking me, Miss Restaurant Critic?"

"The Italian Garden, in Little Italy. It's not far," and off we went.

Over dinner, I made a point of asking about her, avoiding any hint of trying to exalt myself.

She liked baseball and followed the Omaha Cardinals, a St. Louis farm team. She'd grown up with Omaha native Jackie Brandt, now a major leaguer with the Giants, who'd moved to San Francisco in 1958. I told her about flying with Dusty Rhodes, the Giants 1954 World Series hero whose pinch-hit home run had won the game. Sadly, the Omaha team was soon changing to a Dodgers farm team.

I asked the obvious question. "Is Daphne's father still in the picture?" *Here's hoping I have an open field with the lady.* Her one-word answer was delivered with a smile. "Nope."

Dinner, wine and dessert later, I drove Shelley home and walked her to the front door.

"This was a lovely evening, Major, thank you," and with that, she leaned forward and kissed me on the cheek. Not what I was hoping for, but a good start.

"Would you like to do it again?" She answered immediately and with a smile. "Yes, I would."

And we did, on my last night in Omaha. This time Daphne was front and center in the doorway. Shelley stood behind her daughter, applying loving kneading to the child's shoulders and a last hug and kiss before we departed.

Dinner was at Cleo's Nite & Day Bar-B-Q in North Omaha. This was picnic tables covered in newspaper instead of linen tablecloths. She'd picked a spot that showed another side of herself and perhaps showed things she wanted to know about me. So I hoped.

Our conversations were now about her daughter and her job. Dinner was relaxed as my companion smiled and laughed. I'd found a cheerful person who enjoyed life. As I drove her home, I hoped we might move forward with a budding relationship. As I walked her to the door, Shelley turned to face me.

"Red, I know where you hope this is going to go. And before we go any further, I think you should know that I bat for the other team." Her baseball reference confused me. Being a Dodgers fan just showed poor judgment, nothing more. I wasn't getting the message, so she tried again.

"I like girls, Red." My face probably showed stupidity, as I still was missing the point she was laboring to get across. I could see that she loved and doted on her daughter. *That must be it.*

"Red, I'm a lesbian."

My mouth momentarily dropped open momentarily before I recovered my composure. That was not what I'd expected or wanted to hear.

"But you have a daughter." She just shook her head but didn't break eye contact with me.

"Yes, I do, so don't tell me to try it; I might like it. I tried men, but I prefer girls. Sorry."

Then I think I detected a whiff of reproach creeping into her voice.

"You guys, what egos you have, to think that all women find you irresistible."

"Wow," and we both fell into silence. *She was right. I'd been an asshole and I regretted my comment. Perhaps she detected regret, shame or something as I stared down at the floor. But she saved us both by breaking the silence.*

"Listen mister, you are great. You're a gentleman. You're smart and very easy on the eye. I will always be your willing date, if you understand that our evenings end here, at my front door."

As my words continued to fail me, I kissed her hand and silently turned to go.

"Get back here, you lug," and she pulled me into a two-armed hug, kissing me full on the lips. "Thank you for a wonderful evening," then she went inside while I walked to the Buick.

Before leaving Offutt and Omaha, for now at least, I left a box of chocolates on Shelley's desk. My note was simple, "Call me if you switch teams," signed "Bill."

KC-135 Aerial Tanker

The Air Force wanted me to be an air refueling tanker pilot. This job, while not showy, was essential. I suppose I should have seen it as an honor. Two aircraft flying 400 miles an hour less than 50 feet apart was no mean feat. SAC needed to extend the reach of their intercontinental bombers. To Russia and back required over one tank of gas for a B-47 and especially for our new B-52s.

I got orders sending me to Carswell AFB at Fort Worth, Texas, to the 920th Air Refueling Squadron. Why me? People above my pay grade must have seen me as a suitable candidate because I was qualified on jets and multi-engine aircraft and a career officer with over 1,000 hours of flight time.

At Carswell, I got oriented to the new Boeing KC-135 tanker. It can fly at 600 miles per hour, carry 33,000 gallons of fuel and has a range of 5,000 miles fully loaded or over 11,000 miles with a partial fuel cargo.

The trick to piloting one of these is precision flying: to hit and hold an air station and fly steady, straight and level for the whole refueling operation.

* * * *

Was I upset by my experience with Shelley? Hell no. She'd been good company and a wonderful dinner companion. Smart, witty and full of life. What a shame she was gay. So, after my refueling classes at Offutt, I was ready to concentrate on getting into the cockpit of this new bird and taking to the skies.

Designed and built by Boeing, the airframe was the same as their 707 commercial jet, which Pan AM had been flying since 1958. Our KC-135 versions had larger wings and eight feet of added length.

At 320,000 pounds fully loaded with 33,000 gallons of fuel, this would be the heaviest plane I'd ever taken aloft. To get all that weight off the ground, our plane, and all those that came after her, were powered by four of the new Rolls-Royce turbofan engines.

We had no navigator and no ashtrays, just a series of six interconnected fuel bladders. I'd be piloting a gas tank with wings. Even though we came equipped with devices to wick away static electricity, we all wore rubber-soled shoes and avoided metal objects wherever possible.

In our pre-flight briefing, I met my co-pilot, Capt. Gerry Hillyard, waiting with our flying boom operator, TSgt John Stulgis. I recognized Gerry and John from our ground schools, but introduced myself as we stood there, waiting for the briefing to begin.

"Gentlemen, I'm Bill Black, but they call me 'Red.' You can probably guess why. Captain, Tech Sergeant, it's a pleasure. How about we see if this big bastard will fly?

For our flight today, we'd fly unloaded. Once I had the feel of flying the KC-135, then we'd fly with gas aboard. Today we'd practice flight maneuvers for refueling. Tech Sgt. Stulgis would practice telescoping the flying boom and getting it to latch to a fueling port.

My job: to fly straight and level at a constant speed, remembering that I held us only 50 feet away from another aircraft. John's job was to direct the telescoping flying boom that we trailed behind into the fueling ports at the front of all our planes. Hey, we had a fueling port ourselves, so we could be refueled mid-air if need be.

Out on the tarmac, our crew chief and fueling crew chief waited to introduce themselves. We climbed aboard through an access door above the front landing gear bay. I didn't even need a ladder to get in. Wow!

The cockpit instrumentation was nothing new, just more of it. I also had gauges showing the onboard fuel load. The boom operator controlled the actual pumping once he latched the boom into the fueling port. At 6,000 gallons per minute, fueling was shorter than a break-up's last kiss.

With our engines started, I taxied us out and got clearance from the tower to take off. Throttling the four jet engines forward, I found the acceleration smooth as I powered up to full throttle and we lifted off.

Gerry Hillyard raised our landing gear and read off our flight coordinates for today. We'd be meeting up with a T-33 flight trainer. Stulgis now practiced telescoping the boom into the trailing jet's fuel port.

The plane was quiet compared to anything I'd piloted before. There was even room to stand and pass through to the catwalk above the fuel bladders that went all the way to the boom operator's station.

Our plane was pressurized; no air masks required. I had all the power I needed right at my fingertips. The Rolls-Royce engines were smooth, strong and responsive. There was even an autopilot that I could engage, but not during refueling. That was all manual flying, done by me.

We spent three hours in the air. TSgt. Stulgis practiced disengaging the boom from our fuselage and extending it to the customer plane.

The boom operator talked directly with the pilot, guiding him to a final lock of boom and fueling port. I actually had the easier of the two jobs. *I think the autopilot is so I can grab a nap.* Twice more we practice today's exercise without any fuel being transferred.

On day four, we all agreed were ready to do an actual refueling. And we did. A succession of six F-100 Super Sabre Jets bellied up to our bar and drank their fill. We repeated the same scenario twice more in the coming days.

Graduation day came after we successfully fueled planes while a Certifying Officer observed from a chase plane that dogged us from takeoff to landing. We passed and headed back to my new home squadron at Tyndall. Flying one of these enormous birds was not the race car I'd been used to. I could now image myself in a cockpit for a commercial carrier after I retired.

* * * *

Officers don't have a mail call like in the movies. As a permanent party at Tyndall, I had a mailbox at the squadron HQ. A month after Shelley and I parted, there was a letter from Omaha in my mail slot.

"Hello Bill. The next time you are in Omaha, I have a girl for you to meet. And no, she doesn't bat for my team. All the best, love, Shelley."

That was all she wrote. So, what do I think? What do I do?

Here was a woman whom I found attractive in more than physical ways. Smart, happy and funny: three things I wanted in a spouse. Shelley told me I'd been a gentleman whose company she enjoyed. Nothing about her warned me away from following her lead.

I'd just been promoted to Operations Group Commander, XO for short. As the number-two man in the squadron's chain of command, I had a reason, something less than pure bullshit, to travel up to Offutt. Our refueling squadron came under SAC's command, so I actually had regular contact with Omaha. But first I'd write back to Shelley for details.

Who was this woman? Was she single, divorced, or widowed? Kids or no kids? And why did Shelley believe this might be the girl for me? Lots of questions had to be answered before I decided about making the trip to Omaha.

In a week, I had a letter with my answers. Joyce Lester was a secretary at SAC and knew about me because she was the only one who could read my terrible handwriting. She was my age, never married, and had no children. Good at her job and not impressed by hot-shot pilots. She liked to dine and dance, and seemed to be an all-around honest and happy person.

Last on Shelley's list of "Why her?" qualities was, "And she isn't trolling for a husband." I liked the person Shelley described and looked forward to making Joyce's acquaintance.

* * * *

Shelley arranged a double date at Cleo's Bar-B-Q. Shelley came with her partner, Danielle, and I would meet Joyce for the first time over dinner. Cleo's fit the bill because it was about honest food, served in baking pans, enjoyed outside at a picnic table covered in newspaper. Nobody tries to impress somebody by taking them to Cleo's.

"Red, this is Joyce. For your information, she is The Person," Shelley added with great emphasis, "who gives the national press and media Santa's progress from the North Pole on Christmas Eve."

Joyce was slim and wore her chestnut-brown hair in a short bob. Over St. Louis-style barbequed ribs and beer, eaten as neatly as barbequed ribs could be, I got to know a charming, cheerful person.

After the leisurely two hours of food and beer, I asked if anyone would like me to take us all out for ice cream.

Three enthusiastic "Yeses" came back to me. As a visitor to Omaha, I suggested I'd need a guide and navigator.

"Shelley, is this guy safe enough for me to ride with all the way to Ferdinand's Ice Cream?" asked a smiling Joyce.

"I think so." Shelley smiled back in reply. "In the times he took me out, I never had to fight him off." She turned to me in mock seriousness. "So Red, has the arm I twisted fully recovered?" Then, with perfect comic timing, she added, "No, he was a perfect gentleman, which is unusual for fighter pilots."

"Hey, I'm a former fighter pilot, please." Then I waited for a response from Joyce.

"I'll risk riding with the major. But maybe just to be safe, make sure that I show up to work tomorrow, OK?"

We sat outside under Ferdinand's awning on the shop's wrought-iron chairs. Our four cones, in four different flavors of custom-made ice cream, were excellent. Shelley and Danielle let us take the lead in conversations about our jobs and lives before today. Joyce was an Iowa farm girl, so my chicken-farm beginnings were a non-issue for her.

With twilight disappearing and our cones consumed, I asked Joyce if I could drive her home, and she said, "Yes." I followed her directions to a set of one-story apartment units arranged around a central lawn and garden courtyard. Once we were through the wrought-iron gate separating the garden from the sidewalk, the noise of cars disappeared. The sounds of televisions came from behind apartment doors. As we walked to her door, we passed a two-tier fountain decorated in Spanish tile. Its water added a soft background to the electric entertainment sounds escaping from her neighbors' places.

"Thank you for the elegant dinner and fabulous dessert." Her smile never dimmed, and I sensed being gently put on. "I had a wonderful time." And with that, it was my turn.

"May I see you again? I'm in Omaha for another day." And I waited, hoping for a yes.

"Why, Major, I'd like that. Thank you."

"Would tomorrow be too soon?"

"No, not too soon," she smiled back at me.

"Well, okay then, good night."

Joyce turned and went inside, and I walked back to my Buick. I was looking forward to tomorrow.

We were married in September 1961, in her mother's living room in Webster City, Iowa. We remained together and in love for the rest of our lives.

Epilogue

Historians will distill each war into a manageable quantity. They will record and quantify the deaths. How many tons of bombs, bullets and boats were spent on both sides? Regimental and squadron reunions will keep memories alive. The movies will tell just enough truth to tantalize the public. And those of us who lived these sojourns in hell won't talk about what we've seen or done.

What did the war cost us? More than the loss of limbs or lives, it cost us our innocence. I learned to hate people I didn't even know. I learned the world was a dangerous place. And I learned that people I didn't know hated me.

But trained men willing to step into harm's way will always be needed, so here I am.

Lieutenant Colonel William "Red" Black, USAF, Retired

The End

If you enjoyed this book, please do the author and other readers a favor. Go to Amazon or another online retailer and give it a review. Even a star rating would be nice.

Afterword

During my childhood in the 1960s, the Cuban missile crisis was the only time I ever saw or heard my parents outwardly worried about world affairs crashing into our lives. It left an impression on me. It was only much later that we discovered Uncle Bill had been involved.

On April 17, 1961, 1,500 Cuban exiles, equipped by the United States, invaded Cuba hoping to raise a popular rebellion and depose Fidel Castro. Three American war planes, flown by Cuban pilots, led the attack, destroying a portion of Castro's small air force. But promised air support never showed up, and finally the men on the beach succumbed to strafing by the Cuban air force. The Bay of Pigs invasion was a failure

I asked my uncle, "Why did the landing fail?"

"Stu, all I know is, two squadrons of B-26s were supposed to go. One squadron from the States and the second from Central America. And they didn't go."

My research pinned the Alabama Air National Guard as one unit and a CIA group, the other. That President Kennedy called off the air strikes is now confirmed, but why he did it remains lost to the sands of time.

In October 1962, the United States discovered Russia was staging nuclear-capable missiles in Cuba. The Russians did this because we had stationed comparable missiles in Italy and Turkey.

We instituted a Naval blockade and demanded the removal of the missiles. During the 35 days of the crisis, Red Black was the Operations Officer for his refueling squadron. He and the squadron commander took turns flying a KC-135 refueling plane that kept two B-47 bombers continually circling Cuba. What the nuclear-capable bombers carried, he didn't know.

* * * *

In 1965, Red Black piloted one of a series of refueling planes that accompanied groups of six F-100 Super Saber jets from California to Vietnam on an island-hopping route.

Next, he did a tour with the Air Defense Command as an interceptor pilot flying F-102 Delta Daggers out of Thule, Greenland. While there, he played poker in the 'ready room' where pilots waited to take planes into the sky to intercept Russian bombers. He returned from Greenland having won the price of a new Buick convertible.

The news that Ed White, Bill's former roommate from Tyndall, had perished with Roger Chaffee and Gus Grissom in the 1967 NASA Apollo capsule fire reportedly hit Bill hard. I can only estimate the significance of this passing based on how, twenty years later, Bill recalled sharing more than just a residence with Ed White. White's death seemed to somehow connect with the wartime deaths of other friends.

I was looking for a tidy happy ending. I didn't find one. Uncle Bill never got any help for his night terrors and flashbacks. As a result, his marriage and family both paid a price. The stresses continued to add up.

He knew that help was available through the VA. "It might be helpful to some guys," Bill told his wife, "but not for me."
His life finally improved, but only after the passing of his wife in September 1997. The only ray of sunshine was how much peace he found living alone and having regular visits from his daughter. She became a traveling companion and in his later years arranged and monitored his medical and nursing home care.

Bill Black went to war at the age of 18. He became a professional warrior and the product of his life experiences. Those experiences created the man. He was the best husband and father that he could be. But in the end, the only peace he found was in solitude: the same personal solitude that he'd known for his 25 years of war.

Stuart L. Scott

Acknowledgments

I owe a continuing debt to my volunteer Beta readers and my consultants: Dr. Jay Hunter, M.D.; Attorney Duncan Palmatier; David Quinn; Glen Lanier; Kasse Jones; Ted Unzicker; Louise Regelin; Gary and Beverly Fuller; Lynne Whisner; Amy Johnston; Monica Ray; Monique Lillard; Anna Blaisdell and Dave Gressard. I would also be lost without Gordon Long, my editor. They all struggle mightily to save me from my own literary mistakes.

Appendix: B-24 Crew

Here are the names, ranks and duties of the actual crew members of Bill's bomber, according to the records of the American Air Museum in Britain. I could not determine who lived through the war and who didn't make it. The American Museum shows them landing in Sweden, which was where they radioed they were going, not Denmark, where they actually crashed.)

    First Lieutenant Horace Heusen, Pilot
    Second Lieutenant Paul Barrow, Co-Pilot
    Second Lieutenant William Black, Navigator
    Second Lieutenant Robert Bauer, Bombardier
    Technical Sergeant Leon Enloe, Radio Operator
    Technical Sergean Alvin Shaw, Top Turret Gunner
    Staff Sergeant Kenneth Helstrom, Nose Gunner
    Staff Sergeant Milton Shawley, Left Waist Gunner
    Staff Sergeant Ernest Johnson, Tail Gunner
    Staff Sergeant Herbert Hawks, Right Waist Gunner

Bibliography

Carey, Alan C., *Images of War Twin Mustang, The North American F-82 at War*. Pen and Sword Ltd., 2014. South Yorkshire, UK.
Dorr, Robert F., *B-24 Liberator Units of the 8th Air Force*. Oxford Press, 1999. Oxford, UK.
Gladwell, Malcolm, *The Bomber Mafia*. Little, Brown, 2021. New York.
Olson, Lynn, *Citizens of London*. Random House, 2010. New York
O'Rourke, G.G., with Wooldridge, E.T., *Night Fighters over Korea.*1998, published by the authors
Millett, Allan R., *The Korean War*. Potomac Books, 2007. Dulles, VA.

About the Author

After returning from the Air Force, Stuart L. Scott worked as staff in a juvenile detention facility, moved on to adult probation and finally to federal probation and parole. In 1978 he returned to the military as a reserve agent with the Army CID.

Born and raised in the San Francisco Bay area, he has lived with his wife in Moscow, Idaho since 1981. Believing that we only go around once in life and that one job is never enough, his other careers include: professional winemaker, college instructor, director of a school for disabled children and stained-glass artist. His introduction to commercial writing came as an outgrowth of an introduction to the therapeutic value of journaling as part of a Veterans' PTSD counseling group.

SLS@Turbonet.com

Also By This Author

The Tooth Fairy
A story as cold as a Spokane winter about what happens when a crook chooses the wrong victim.
The Grand Tetons
The Texas bank robber who carries twin 38's.
Idaho Catch and Release
Husband and wife pornographers who give a new meaning to what's really a crime.
The Deal
The 1976 case of a crooked politician revisited in 2016.

Available at most online retailers
ISBN:9781732246812

Sample from *Gritty, Grisly, Greedy*

The Grand Tetons

It was a hot August day in 1969 when Janet Lee walked into the center of Clarksville, Texas from where she parked her car in the Seven Eleven lot by the highway. Her hometown in Oklahoma looked just like this one. The square of every small Texas town had either a courthouse or a city hall on one side. Across the square was the bank, and between the two, in the center of the square, was a flagpole with a cannon at its base. The red, white and blue of the Texas flag hung just below Old Glory. With no breeze, the two flags blended into one mass of colors.

"I wonder if this is the Clarksville that The Monkees sang about?" she muttered as she crossed the square. The Walmart that had come to town last year had already driven out many of the local merchants. The storefronts on the square were all empty except for the Farmers and Merchants Bank. That was all she needed. It was more than that. It was a gift, and you could make more of it.

Entering the bank, Janet let her eyes adjust to the interior lighting. A manager sat at a desk in the rear of the lobby. She doodled on a withdrawal slip before taking it over to the lone teller who stood at one of the three stations.

"Hello." She switched on her most dazzling smile, tossed her ash-blond hair and beamed at the young man with her bright blue eyes.

"Good morning, Ma'am." He flushed. "Ar…eh…I mean good afternoon." He finally managed to get out, "How can I help you today?"

"Well thank you." She smiled and passed the withdrawal slip across the counter. "I'd like to make a withdrawal, please."

Slowly she opened the front of her short denim jacket, first one side and then the other, to reveal the white fishnet of her tank top. The smile on the face of the young man disappeared.

His eyes were drawn to the rose-pink nipples that seemed to be staring at him through the mesh. He tried looking back up to her brilliant smile but couldn't. From her round, firm breasts the rosy nipples were still staring up at his eyes. Then his gaze dropped to the large brown wood gun butt that hugged the flat of her stomach. Some emblem, a Texas star perhaps, was inset on the grip.

"Take all the money from your drawer and put it in the bag, honey." She held eye contact with him, even though his stare had not yet left the gun. She removed a white flour sack from her back pocket and passed it across the counter. "Please don't spoil either of our days by pushing any alarm. Momma needs the money for her surgery, and I'm just trying to be a good daughter."

When the full bag slid back across the counter, she spoke again. "Wait just a bit before you do anything." She did her best to portray both innocence and vulnerability by managing a small frown. Then, buttoning the middle button on her jacket, she walked out of the bank, but not out of his dreams.

* * * *

"So can you tell me what she was wearing?" asked Deputy Sheriff Muldrow, from Red River County.

"Denim jeans and a denim jacket," was the response. The answer from the teller started the deputy writing in his notebook as they sat across the table in the bank's employee lounge.

"What color was her hair?"

"I don't remember." The teller stared at the table, avoiding eye contact with the deputy.

"What about the color of her eyes?"

"I don't remember." The deputy pressed on.

"Did she have a gun?"

"Yes, there was a gun."

At last, they we're back on track. "Okay, what kind of a gun was it?"

"Big gun." He shook his head apologetically.

Trying not to let his frustration show, the deputy tried again. "Is there anything else you can recall?" The teller didn't seem to hear the question. After what seemed like a minute, Muldrow repeated the question.

"She had a beautiful smile. I just couldn't seem to tear my eyes away."

"From her smile?"

"Yes, that's right, from her smile." Then he shut up. He wasn't about to volunteer that all he could recall were her beautiful breasts.

Prisoners of War is simultaneously a love story, a mystery and a history, all woven together. Everything of a historical nature is true to the best of my knowledge and research. Conflict between love and duty. Conflict between love of country and the love of your life. How far would you go to win back your love, when the government has taken her away? Fear, racism and abiding love collide in 1942 America, when your only crime was being born Japanese.

Kirkus review says, "The author has a gift for sympathetic portrayal of antagonistic views."
and
"An affecting, historically keen story."

Available at most online retailers
ISBN: 978-1-7322468-2-9

Sample from Prisoners of War

Chapter 1: Keyport, 1941

It was late the morning of December 7 when I heard a commotion at the Olson house next door—crying and swearing. It sounded like a family fight, loud and vulgar even, yet personal. Sounds of confusion were also coming from the main gate at the nearby Keyport, Washington, Torpedo Station. I was used to the noise in the Keyport machine shop where I worked, building torpedoes for the Bureau of Ordinance. This was a different sound. Trucks were moving, people were shouting and booted feet were running. Behind me, through his closed door, I heard my roommate Duano's voice.

"God damn it, you guys!"

He emerged half-dressed with jeans and socks on, his shirt and shoes in hand.

"Sunday morning is supposed to be quiet, Pat. What is the problem with those assholes?"

"Come on. Get dressed, and we'll head over to the gate and see what's up."

We walked out past our neighbor's store and into the street. Up ahead, one of the many Marines standing around turned briefly to respond to our shouted question.

"What the hell's going on?"

"The Japs bombed our fleet at Pearl Harbor. We're at war."

His words stopped us both in our tracks. In the confusion at the main gate, I saw a familiar figure, Captain Olson, my landlord and chief of security at Keyport.

"Captain Olson! Is there something we should do to help? Just tell us what you need."

"Thanks, McBride. For now, it would be best for you just to go home until your next shift. If I need to organize work or defense parties, I'll send someone over to get you. Bad business, this."

Then Olson turned away to direct the makeshift barricade being erected outside the gate. Still stunned, Duano and I walked back to our house and sat down on the porch to watch the action at the main gate. I stepped inside and turned on the radio, hoping for, all the while dreading, more news.

The news was on every station. The few details available were being repeated and occasionally augmented when more information came in from across the Pacific. We didn't have a phone, so I tried calling home using the pay phone at the Keyport Mercantile. Again and again, I turned the rotary dial, trying to call San Bruno. I tried my parents' house first and then my fiancée's home, but every attempt rang as a busy signal.

Walking away from the pay phone through the bright sun of this particular Sunday morning, I would never have believed that inside of two years I would become a traitor to my country.

Meet the three women who turn the tables on their victimizers; the bigamist, the rapist and the molester.

"A deceptively slim yet viciously potent slice of female retribution." Kirkus Reviews

Available at most online retailers
ISBN: 978-1-7322468-6-7

Sample from Spirit Lake Payback

Prologue: Spokane, Washington

June 6, 1995

The Spokane newspaper article ran under the banner, **Residents Rush to Plug Leaky Lake.**

"It was only last week that this reporter's boat was in the water, but now it's beached on weeds and mud, here next to my dock. State officials aren't sure why the lake is leaking, but they know it's leaking a lot of water into the Spokane aquifer. The state believes that holes are the main problem. The spokesman for the Idaho Department of Lands explained. 'It's tough to tell legitimate holes from the occasional moose footprint, or one dug by a toad when the lakebed was dry. The trick is to stir up some muck near a suspected hole. If it gets sucked down, the hole is declared a "leaker" and resealed. Unless you see it happen, it's hard to believe.'"

June 10, 1995

Today the follow-up newspaper headline was an eye catcher. **Spirit Lake Sink Hole Collapses to Reveal Skeletal Remains.**

"Idaho authorities interrupted the efforts of local homeowners to seal the continuing plague of sink holes when an undetermined number of human skeletons were discovered in the bottom muck of a collapsed sink hole. A 250 ft. area on the south shore of the lake has been cordoned off. State and tribal archeologists are preparing to excavate the site, hoping to determine the provenance of the apparent ancient burial ground."

June 30, 1995

Spirit Lake Sink Hole Linked to Mob Body Dump.

The Kootenai County Sheriff in his lakeside press conference revealed, "Those remains appear to be 40 to 60 years old and not a tribal burial ground as we first imagined. The archeological excavation has yielded up scraps of clothing and shoes that confirm the approximate age of the remains. The Coeur d'Alene tribal Archeologist called us in yesterday when he removed a skull from the pit and noticed fillings and gold teeth. Once the site is excavated, the identification of the remains will begin. Until that time, we have a bit of a mystery on our hands."

A combined local, state and federal multi-agency task force recovered nine bodies from their Spirit Lake dump site. Skeletal remains had become disarticulated into a pile of anonymous bones, awaiting re-assembly. When they were dumped was a mystery, but bullet holes in many of the skulls and cut marks on bones all pointed to violent ends for the nine unknowns.

Before COVID-19 was the 1918 Spanish Flu. Before that was the 1916 Polio epidemic. New York City had the highest infection rate, but the state with the worst rate was Nevada.

The last US Mail wagon robbery in the country happened in Nevada and the stolen payroll money was never found. To boost his newspaper sales, Joe Pulitzer sent staff West to cover this incident.

Was there a connection?

Available at most online retailers
ISBN: 978-1-7375429-1-9

Sample from Last Ghost Dance

Love and Death in a Small Town

Verrall Black sprang from the swarthy, dark *Reivers* of the Scottish Lowlands, a place of constant border warfare. His beard matched the black of his hair and eyes. He stood 5 foot 9 inches tall, wire tough, the sinews of his forearms bulging beneath their canopy of black hair. His coloration lived on in his oldest daughter, Melba. His second child, Doris, had her mother's red hair and pale skin that would too soon freckle.

The Black family came to Nevada in the 1880s. Verrall Black used the proceeds from his family's success in cattle ranching to open a store in Deeth. The sign above the porch overhang read, "Deeth Mercantile—General Merchandise." The town boasted 500 souls in 1908, and his was the only store. The local Paiute band sold pine nuts and deer hide gloves to the mercantile.

Business was good, supplying the locals from Starr Valley, miners from the gold mines at Jarbidge, and cowboys from The Union Land and Cattle Company that ran over 1,000 head of cattle on the sage-covered range surrounding the town.

Across the dirt street from the Mercantile was the Post Office. As the railhead for the Jarbidge mines, Deeth became the largest town in Northern Nevada. Jarbidge gold fueled an expanding local economy.

An opera house, roller rink, barbershop and ice cream parlor opened. Solidifying Deeth as a town was a two-cell city jail, a one-room school, a Chinese laundry and a boarding house and restaurant.

The boarding house was not to be confused with the "Women's Boarding House" that operated above the town's only tavern and dance hall, owned by John Hudson. Cowboys, miners and railroad men now had more opportunities to shed

their burden of heavy gold coins. Three "working ladies," Minnie, Mabel, and Lottie, rented the rooms upstairs. Hudson was their landlord, not their employer.

Lottie Loomis was a willowy brunette from California. She had left her home heading for Denver but only made it as far as Deeth. She had the looks, personality and discipline to do more than trade what she had for what she needed to get by; she aspired to operate a house of her own. She exuded seduction along with raw sexuality. Lottie's real talent was effortlessly convincing men that she wanted them as much as they wanted her. She flirted. She teased. She told every man that found his way into her arms, "You are different from all the men I've known before." Unfortunately, John Hudson believed her.

The saloon owner had set his sights on Lottie. He dreamed about her constantly, in fantasies both erotic and domestic. He took every opportunity to keep her in his sight. Lacking self-esteem, he never risked the rejection, or worse, ridicule by showing his feelings.

John had a hired bartender in the evening, allowing him to float between being a greeter and piano player. As he played his piano below, his mind couldn't escape the thought of Lottie in bed with another man just above him. One Saturday night, he watched Lottie ascend the stairs with a customer, laughing and smiling at the man. His control cracked. His eyes leaked tears as he played the ivory keys. Onward his imagination led him. She was up there now, right above his head, sharing her charms with someone who didn't love her or deserve her as he did.

His hands balled into fist and the fists crashed onto the keyboard. The clang of the keys rang out over the conversations from the barroom and dance floor. As the music stopped, so did the dancers and the talk. The room went silent when John drew out a Colt revolver from his inside coat pocket and began shooting into the dance hall ceiling. "Boom-boom-boom."

No one moved. One group of four men immediately turned their table sideways for a barricade. Ben Kuhl, a small-time thief, had just introduced his two friends, Bob McGinty and Ed Beck, to Fred Searcy, a local teamster. Kuhl believed Fred, who drove a freight wagon, might be a good man to know. He'd file away Searcy's name and his job for possible later use.

The four looked over the table top. Every eye in the room was now focused on Hudson. Adjusting his aim, he let loose again, "boom-boom-boom," emptying his gun into the pale plaster ceiling. The crowd watched as he turned away from the piano and dropped the pistol onto the floorboards at his feet. His elbows went to his knees as he wept into his hands. Drops of smelly liquid began to fall through the bullet holes and drip onto his shirt.

Ed Smiley, the bartender, finally judged it safe to approach his sobbing boss. He picked up the gun, passing it to Dennis McDermott. Ed then walked through the cloud of black powder smoke and climbed the stairs from the dance hall to the bedrooms. From the hallway, the two other doors were cracked open. Other upstairs customers, half-clad, peeked out. The door to Lottie's room was still shut. Ed paused at the door, listening. Finally, he spoke the first words since the shooting. "I'm coming in."

No one was alive inside the small room. Two naked figures lay entangled on the metal-framed bed. Lottie's body lay face down astride her male guest. Blood pooled on the bedding and the floor from two bullet wounds to her upper body. Her companion was shot in the thigh. Other wound tracks, concealed by their bodies, were dripping blood onto the floor. There it mixed with the liquid contents of a chamber pot under the bed, also shot through. The ammonia from urine mixed with the iron smell of their blood.

Ed backed up, closed the door and walked down the stairs to the dance hall.

Hudson was still seated on his piano stool, head in hands. Word had spread out from the bar to the de facto leaders of the town. Verrall Black, Ben Armstrong and Bob Anderson clustered together with Dennis McDermott in the center of the room.

Ed took two steps toward the men before speaking. "Lottie and Roy Wooden, the section foreman, are both dead." Standing aside as the four men whispered among themselves, Smiley posed the unspoken question on many minds. "What's to be done now?"

Verrall Black spoke for the group. "We've been talking it over. Ben and Bob will take Hudson over to the jail for the night. We'll ask Mabel and Minnie to clean up Lottie's body and wind her tight in a sheet. You and I will do the same for Roy."

"Then what?" asked Ed.

"You get some help, maybe the other men upstairs, and move the two bodies to the cattle company shed for now. That will keep them cold and safe until somebody comes up from Elko."

Smiley nodded his agreement. The five men separated to deal with their appointed tasks. Hudson's shirt was soaked by the drops falling from above. Fate had pissed on him again.

As they separated, one of the group turned and stopped the bartender with a question." Did she know how he felt?"

"I guess not."

Later Saturday night, Verrall and Ed Smiley took two blankets, a plate of biscuits and stew, hard candy and a cup of hot coffee over to John Hudson. They had no concerns about Hudson trying to escape.

"John, these should help you through the night. There's a slop bucket under the bunk. You may have already found that."

Hudson nodded that he had. He sat on the wooden bunk, staring at the cement floor, but neither spoke nor made eye contact with Black.

Verrall nudged Hudson with the plate and offered the hot cup of coffee. Hudson took both as Ed Smiley entered the cell and placed the blankets on the bunk.

As the cell door closed, Hudson looked up and gave a momentary smile. "Thank you." After a long pause, he spoke again. "They're dead, aren't they." It was not a question.

Ed Smiley delivered the answer as the cell door closed. "Yes. Both."

In the morning, John Hudson was dead by his own hand, hung with an improvised noose fashioned from strips of blankets braided together and attached to bars in the cell window. His meager last meal lay untouched on the bunk.

www.ingramcontent.com/pod-product-compliance
Lightning Source LLC
Chambersburg PA
CBHW072050110526
44590CB00018B/3112